CREATING SKETCHBOOKS

FOR EMBROIDERERS AND TEXTILE ARTISTS

Kay Greenlees

BATSFORD

CREATING SKETCHBOOKS

FOR EMBROIDERERS AND TEXTILE ARTISTS

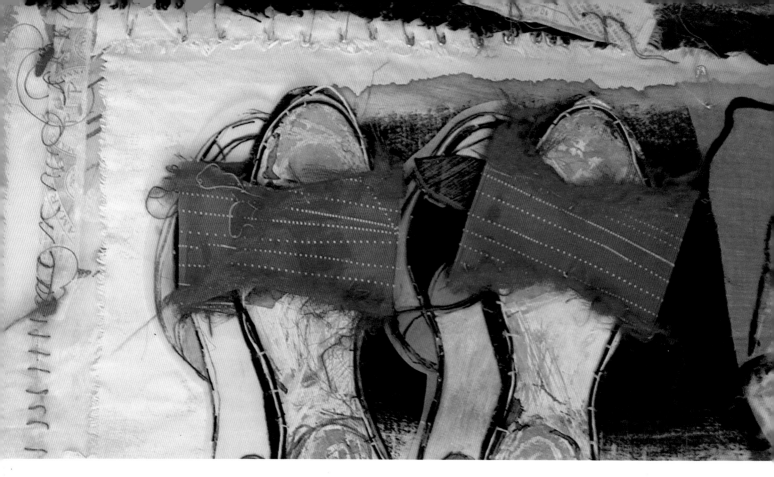

Previous page:

Greek sketchbook: Burnt Grass and Light

Julia Caprara

A3 (297 x 420mm [11¾ x 16½in])

Above:

Untitled (detail)

Sally E Payne

Mixed media, calico, painting, screen printing,
paper, stitch, photographs, inks

Photography: Sally E Payne

First published in the United Kingdom in 2005 by
Batsford
10 Southcombe Street
London W14 0RA
An imprint of Anova Books Company Ltd

ISBN 9780713489576

A CIP catalogue record for this book is available from the British Library.

15 14 13 12

10

Printed by Craft Print International Limited, Singapore

This book can be ordered direct from the publisher at the website:
www.anovabooks.com, or try your local bookshop

Distributed in the United States and Canada by Sterling Publishing Co.,
387 Park Avenue South, New York, NY 10016, USA

Photography by Michael Wicks unless specified otherwise.

CONTENTS

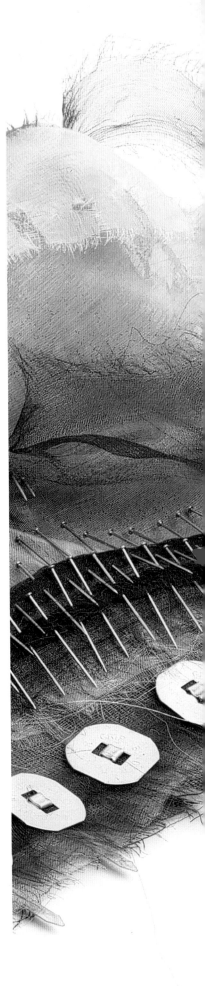

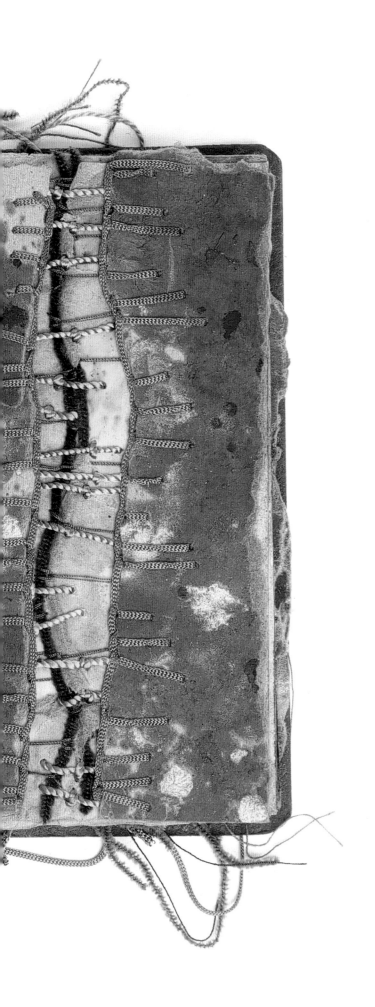

DEFINING THE FIELD

What is a sketchbook?

It may seem strange to have to ask the question 'what is a sketchbook?', because there are many different ideas about what the word means. The range of interpretations can be confusing and off-putting. Sketchbooks should be both enjoyable and serious. They require a degree of commitment from the beginner that may be quite daunting at first. Perhaps the white pages look too pristine, or what about mistakes? The most common cause for concern is the assumption that sketchbooks are full of drawings and that you have to be 'good' at drawing in order to get started.

What should be in a sketchbook? Regular sketchbook users always seem to take the practice for granted; it's often a habit that has become second nature – so easy and comfortable that the book over time becomes an old friend and its loss can be devastating.

It is the aim of this book to present some answers to these questions by reviewing a range of sketchbook approaches taken by different textile artists. Ideally, this will help you to feel comfortable with your own personal approach and consider ways of reviewing and developing this. Perhaps the most essential point about sketchbooks is that they should be personal to the maker.

Sketchbooks may usefully be called other things. Common alternative names are: journals, notebooks, visual ideas books, visual diaries or workbooks. Within this book, all of these alternatives are embraced by the term *sketchbook*. For an individual artist, designer or maker, however, there may be important and significant differences in the use of a specific name. Many of the artists featured here prefer not to use the term *sketchbook*. Choose what suits you and make the book your own.

Themed sketchbook: rusted surfaces
Kay Greenlees
A6 (105 x 148 mm [4¼ x 5¾ in])
Inks, wax, thread

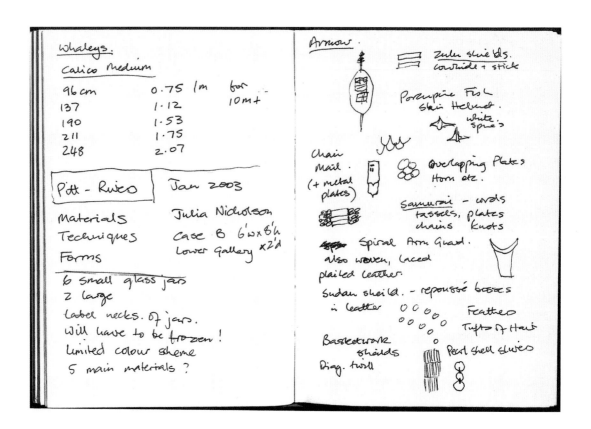

Notebook

Penny Burnfield

A6 (105 x 148 mm [4¼ x 5¾ in])

What is a sketch?

There are a number of synonyms for the word *sketch*, some of which can be helpful in clarifying the intention behind the practice, for example: *outline, draft, skeleton, explanation, illustration, summary, drawing, design, representation, scrawl, scribble, doodle, write, jot, arrange, map* or *set out*. It is clear that for an artist (or writer, or musician), this stage of work is usually an early period of working or investigation that can include a great deal of freedom and excitement. In a visual situation, work must sometimes be undertaken within a limited timescale and is necessarily incomplete and unresolved. The resultant lack of resolution is often equated in a derogatory sense with *quick, rough,* or *ill-considered* rather than with the more positive corollaries, such as *lively, spontaneous, early, considered, deliberate, careful* and *studied*.

Working methods

Sketchbooks can contain a variety of working methods, but the most useful personal books are centred on first-hand observation or investigation. This offers insight, understanding and knowledge that can be referenced in the future. Simple drawings and annotations can contain more information than a snapshot and are therefore more useful than photographs. Although a supporting photograph album may be useful, even brief drawings and written notes will have prompted closer observation and for a more sustained time than photography; this will help you to develop increasingly more acute observational skills.

Sketchbooks may contain any or all of the following:

- Quick drawings and notes
- Flowers, leaves, feathers and other natural forms of interest
- Careful observations and recordings
- Poems or other written pieces
- Pieces of fabric and thread
- Technical information – how things may join, move or fasten, how colours mix
- Found items, such as tickets, wrappers, or cuttings
- Design development
- Textile samples – direct development on or with fabric and design development
- Supporting photography
- Annotations, measurements, instructions
- Targets, action plans

The sketchbook can be used to record all sorts of ideas and feelings, and thoughts about people, places and things. It becomes a unique way of exploring and storing information, including whatever arouses curiosity and interest.

Many people say they find it hard to draw and wish that they were 'better at it'. This sort of comment reveals a preconceived notion about what constitutes a 'good' drawing. If you identify with this, it is useful to try to be a little more analytical about what you mean. Are you seeking more accuracy with scale and form or perhaps a truer likeness? Do you want to create more mood and atmosphere? Are you looking for more accurate perspective? If you need support or enjoy working in the company of others, there is a wide range of books and videos, evening and holiday classes that can offer information on how to draw. However, nothing beats the old adage 'practice makes perfect', and the regular use of a sketchbook offers a good opportunity to go back and review your own development over time.

Why use a sketchbook?

Given that we have already acknowledged that some of us experience a degree of trepidation about starting a sketchbook, or about our skills in drawing, why do we do it? Why do textile courses promote the use of a sketchbook as good practice? What are the benefits of developing this way of working?

A sketchbook will provide:

- A library of responses to experiences as well as information about people, places and things that can inform future reference
- An opportunity to record ideas and images in the form of drawings and notes
- An opportunity to make a variety of personal evaluations and analyses
- Clarity of vision, refinement, simplification

- Fluency of thought and understanding
- Development of memory and imagination
- Identification of problems or possibilities
- Resolution of problems
- Development of the individual artist's vocabulary
- Stimulation and development of ideas
- A trigger for memory or association that links earlier experiences and suggests further ideas and developments

Taking all the above points into consideration when you are working will enable you to create a sketchbook of substance, which has personal meaning and value, recording as it does your own thoughts, images, recollections, observations and engagement with ideas or media. The sketchbook represents a commitment to discovery and investigation or a search for meaning that transcends the notions of triviality that are sometimes associated with 'quick' sketches. Even though one of the main uses of the sketchbook is to allow space for this sort of immediate or spontaneous work, working quickly should not be associated with a casual attitude or lazy observation.

Themed sketchbook: cacti
Linda Livesey
A4 (210 x 297 mm [8¼ x 11¾ in])
Ink, bleach

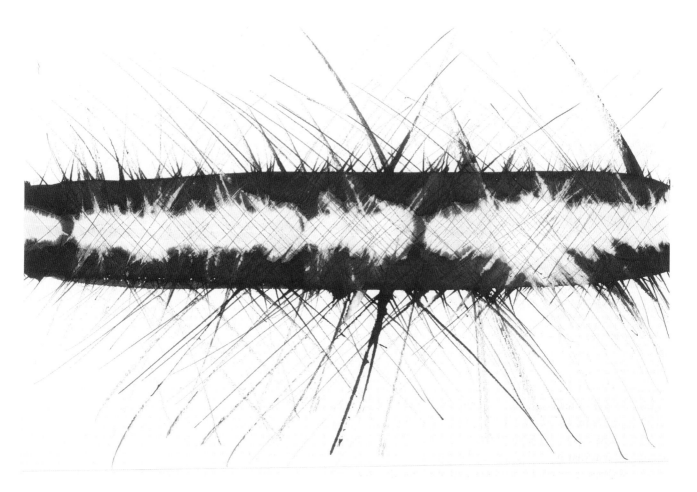

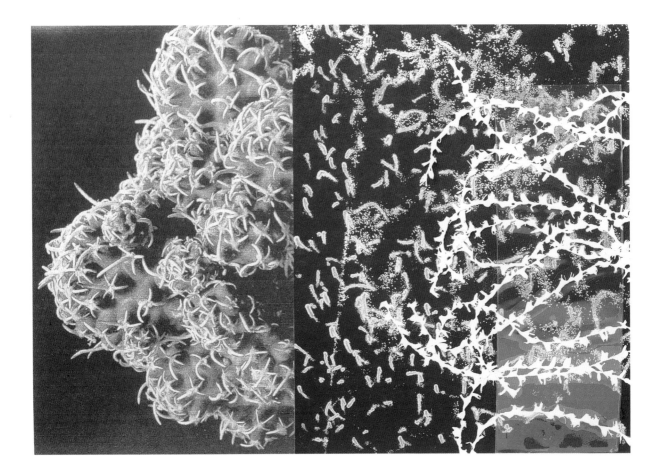

Working with a sketchbook can imbue your work with depth, energy, rigour and significance through:

- Varied and lively content – not just drawings of landscapes or buildings but other drawings (for example of details or made objects), plus cuttings, found objects, comments and annotations
- Exploration of the visual language of art, such as line, shape, colour, tone, texture, pattern and form
- Understanding of space and distance and their relationship
- Experimentation with varied media

While this introduction makes it evident that drawing is an important component of sketchbook work, it should also be understood that different types of drawing are part of the sketching process. If drawing is not for you, then there are many other exciting possibilities open to you. Written journals also serve as a significant way of recording and communicating thoughts, ideas and feelings. Fabric samples may support a distinctive way of working. Sketchbooks, in whatever forms you choose, offer so much potential for individual development and enjoyment that it would be a shame not to make full use of them. The next section outlines some of the purposes that sketchbooks serve.

Themed sketchbook: cacti
Linda Livesey
A4 (210 x 297 mm [8¼ x 11¾ in])
Photocopy reference, monoprint

remnants
fragments
debris
remains
offcuts
sweepings
leftovers
left behind

CHAPTER ONE

PURPOSES OF A SKETCHBOOK: Pause, record, reflect, move on...

So far, I have remarked broadly on why we use sketchbooks and why, in a general sense, they are of value to all individual artists, designers or makers. Having considered the opportunities that using a sketchbook offers and the working methods that contribute to this development, it is worth considering briefly the purposes that sketchbook practice can serve.

I have used the terms *vision* and *re-vision* to encompass both the breadth of possibilities and the spirit of working in a creative and personal way. *Vision* moves beyond the straightforward description of 'to have sight', to include the more creative and personal use of imagination, insight, expression, revelation and the realms of dreaming and fantasy. *Re-vision* simply means 'to look again' or to examine or re-visit and refine ideas and thoughts.

It is fairly easy to list some of the purposes served by the sketchbook (see page 9). What is not easy is to tease these issues apart in order to talk about them, because in reality they overlap or appear in a variety of combinations. Nor do they have a particular order of importance, and for this reason I have chosen to present the possibilities in alphabetical form. This offers a fairly comprehensive list of purposes, to which you can add your own. In reality, all of these purposes might be served by your sketchbooks. The emphasis may vary from book to book, project to project or from time to time. You may move from a time of deep introspection and subjectivity to a more analytical and objective study. What matters is that the approach to the sketchbook work is personal to you.

Sketchbook
Jan Miller
A4 (210 x 297 mm [8¼ x 11¾ in])
Costume study – paper used as analogy for textile
Photography: Jerry Hardman-Jones

Vision and *re-vision* offers the potential to; to have; or to be:				
A	adventure	analyse	assimilate	archive
B	begin	build		
C	communicate challenge	curiosity creative	collect contemplate	critique
D	develop	design	draw	dream
E	experiment explain	engage examine	explore express	evaluate
F	fantasies	fears	fun	
G	generate			
H	hypothesize			
I	imagination invent	inspiration ideas	interpret illustrate	investigate intuition
J	journey			
K	keep			
L	look	linger		
M	memory	move on		
N	narrate	negotiate		
O	observation	ownership		
P	practice play	personal pause	perception	plan
Q	question			
R	research remember	reference reflect	respond re-vision	record
S	sketch sustain synthesize	see specify speculate	sense simplify	select symbolize
T	treasure try	technical	testing	transform
V	vision	visualize		
W	**what if?**			
Y	**you can do it!**			

There is no right or wrong way to use a sketchbook. Even if your sketchbook is part of a textile course, *it is valuable precisely because it records your own personal thoughts, images, recollections, observations and engagement with ideas, experiences and media.*

If the concepts *vision and re-vision* encapsulate the purposes of the sketchbook, then *pause, record, reflect, move on…* can be seen to encapsulate the *actions* required to take part in sketchbook practice. How long you pause for, what form your reflection takes, how you choose to record and at what point you move on will depend on personal circumstances and intentions. While you are still developing your sketchbook practice or if you feel that your current approach is too narrow, it might be worth considering the following information for its potential benefit to your way of working.

Reviewing the purposes that your sketchbook serves for you may help organize or clarify your thoughts. Have a look through your book and try to spot your strengths. A review may leave you worried that you do not have any 'vision' or technical experiments, or it may leave you feeling low in confidence if you can only see a few of the purposes as already described reflected in your own practice. If this is the case, look again at the statement at the bottom of the alphabetical list and look at the sketchbook pages featured in this book. How many of them demonstrate, on any one page, more than a few of the approaches mentioned above?

I have grouped these purposes in pairs or threes, although this choice is to some extent random and it would be easy to offer alternative groupings without losing coherence. For instance, ideas, development and analysis could easily combine. Sketchbook practice should be flexible. There is no intention to suggest that your sketchbook should be prescriptive, or conversely that there is anything to worry about if all of the purposes are covered in each of your sketchbooks. As the purposes of a sketchbook are many and varied, and above all personal, it is worth stating that the categories identified below are grouped for the benefit of talking about them. It is important to 'be yourself'. The headings are intended to prompt discussion and to enable you to review your personal practice more easily.

Observing, recording and storing

Sketching or drawing from observation does not have to mean making an exact copy of what you see, but is a way of encouraging us to look at and understand the world. In the caves at Lascaux and Altamera, for example, are some of the earliest drawings used by people to make representations of the world around them. As well as recording the immediate world, these drawings may well also have had magical or totemic significance.

Drawings or sketches can also be used to record experiences and feelings, as in those by Rozanne Hawksley on pages 22 and 61. Recording can be from direct observation, from memory or from imagination. Recording from direct observation often provides an indispensable basis for further work. It is possible to record from observation in many ways: in words, in pictures, whether drawn or photographed, in diagrams and through textiles. You may decide to use only one or two of these methods or you may combine them. Some artists, such as Andy Goldsworthy, use natural materials, such as rock, mud and snow, in response to their world. Many of the more ephemeral creations are also recorded photographically. The drawings by Jan Miller on pages 12 and 59 record the deterioration of an old and worn garment. Papers have been used as an analogy for textile and marks have been recorded directly in stitch. The narrative linking the pieces is evident throughout the sketchbook.

Alternatively, your recording and observations may be made in a written journal or diary that is also illustrated. There are several examples of 'written' journals in this book, some of which include 'thumbnails' (brief written descriptions) or other contextual research. You could draw in a specific manner, for instance just using line drawings. Compare, for example, the use of line by David Hockney in *Travels with Pen, Pencil and Paint* with that used by Henry Moore in his *Sheep Sketchbook*. Observing and recording will almost certainly lead to other purposeful forms of study, such as exploring, finding different ways to use line or defining the form of the object in three dimensions, or exploring a concept, such as 'relationships'. Observing means that one is looking closely and purposefully at things; making an observational drawing means obtaining and communicating knowledge. Keeping these observations in your sketchbook means that they are available for future re-vision and reference.

Storing information can happen in a variety of ways. Once you have recorded something on a page, even if it is just a mark, it remains 'stored' and as long as you keep the sketchbook it provides a record of a particular moment – a mark on a particular journey. One of the main functions of a sketchbook is to keep these records – random, arbitrary or focused – so that they can be available for future reference. Used in this way, the storage facility of a sketchbook is largely there as a by-product of keeping the book and is one of its many essential features. A collection of sketches by Audrey Walker exemplifies some of these points (see left). The studies have initially been made in different sketchbooks and put together as a sheet of related ideas. In the top left sketch, she has observed and quickly recorded a rock formation that looked like two heads. The other sketches show two further 'thoughts' about this formation and reflect a longstanding interest in heads.

Rock formation/heads
Audrey Walker
220 x 260mm (8¾ x 10¼in)
One sheet of related ideas: a rock formation that looked like two heads, plus thoughts about related heads.

Drawing
Ruth Issett
Collage
Photography:
Kevin Mead

Opposite:
Sketchbook page
Kay Greenlees
A4 (210 x 297mm [8¼ x 11¾in])
Museum studies/samples

Sometimes a sketchbook can be used to keep work that has been started elsewhere. I have one in which I store my experiments from various workshops that I have attended. I normally describe it as a 'workbook' rather than a sketchbook. At times, classes, talks and exhibitions will have no apparent relevance, but at a later stage the pieces will often fall into place and, having secured the material 'in storage', it is available for reconsideration. The book is used as a library of ideas, experiences, contacts, developments, resource lists and starting points. Some of this I will return to, some I'm sure I never will, but just in case… the work remains in place. Additionally, the book also acts as a 'curriculum vitae', reflecting a sustained and committed attitude to personal development as well as a joy and enthusiasm for new learning in the company of others. Equally, a sketchbook could store collections of any number of visual phenomena: letterforms or calligraphy, a library of textures, groups of experimental samples, or mixtures of all these things.

Sketchbook page
Kay Greenlees
A4 (210 x 297mm [8¼ x 11¾in])
Museum studies/samples

Researching and collecting

Research may, of course, be entirely visual, but I have included here examples that use written notes as well as brief annotations. Some pages from a sketchbook are shown that explore textile work from different parts of the world. This kind of research is a requirement common to many different textile courses and levels of study where historical or cultural examples provide a wider context for understanding textile practice. The balance of written, drawn and photographic work should be individual to each student. The purpose you have in carrying out the research may also determine the approach that you take. Sketchbook pages here show sketches from exhibits in a museum, associated notes from various sources, photographs and other secondary resource material, including small contemporary and historical samples.

Finding Indian textile work too large an area, I selected hats and bags as the focus for the study. This, however, could have been narrowed further, perhaps to just hats from a particular region or religion, costume or technique. Many kinds of tassels or pompoms can be seen here that could have provided a stimulating source for ideas, as could the study of a particular stitch, colour combination, textile technique or garment form. In this example, development work is contained within these pages, but not actually resolved in this notebook. These pages are also examples of sustained study in a museum or at an exhibition rather than quick sketches, as discussed on page 88 and shown in the illustrations on page 90.

Sketchbook: Edge qualities

Jo Owen

430 x 180mm (17 x 7in)

2004

Edges, overlapping, layers, cut-outs

In the sketchbook by Jo Owen (above), the purpose of the research was to explore the edge qualities suggested by the costume she saw. Her book is purely about the development of that interest and is completely visual. The point, once again, is to recognize different approaches and select the ones that suit you at a particular point in time. Examples of sketchbook work by Ros Chilcot (pages 74–75) and Julia Caprara (pages 78–79) illustrate other ways in which the research may also be purely visual.

Collecting is probably already a habit with many readers of this book, and many collections will eventually grow beyond the physical capacity of a sketchbook to support. Sketchbooks are obviously most useful for flatter, smaller, collections of a more visual nature. Depending on the size of the objects and the need for protection, most collectors I know utilize bags, boxes and tins as the collection grows. Along with many others, I incorporate collections into final pieces of work. Many people augment their sketches with material that they find along the way, and this in itself may develop into a fascination with newly discovered materials or ideas. Tickets – travel tickets, entry tickets, stamped, punched, clipped and torn tickets – are common. Other items might include

Poppy seed heads – Each drawing got progressively larger and would fit less and less easily –

Like the idea of using the colour of the seed heads as the background colour is shown up the spaces between the seed heads

Sketchbook: Poppy seed heads
Rose Horspool
A5 (148 x 210mm [5¾ x 8¼in])
Coloured pencil, rollerball pen

street litter, sweet wrappers, and graphic items from popular culture or the supermarket, CD store, stationers or card shops. All are suitable, as well as the more common natural forms, such as leaves, flowers and feathers. Once bitten by the collecting bug, variations on the theme begin to be seen in many places. A small incidental collection can soon develop into a major theme, providing inspiration for many starting points or even many years of work. Alternatively, the collection may consist of things you have made yourself. Customized papers can be worked onto, for example, and they might be collected either for their own sake or to serve as a technical record of how they were made. This could also apply to collections of samples that may also be a form of storage, research and experimentation.

Expressing and imagining

Sketchbooks provide some artists with great personal freedom. They work in their books as and when they choose, often every day, finding a personal space for individual responses and expression. Sometimes, the work is intuitive and may explore inner feelings, thoughts and moods that cannot always be readily voiced in other ways. In very different, but equally moving drawings – 'Like a bit of old washing' (below) and 'In grief' (page 61) – Rozanne Hawksley graphically expresses how she felt at a particularly sad time in her life. These pieces are purely emotional and have been worked on for about 15 minutes at a time. She says 'It occurs to me when I feel the need to express something through drawing, that the drawing is an entity in itself – it exists as a drawing, and is my decided response to a situation or a search for a resolution; this can be purely for a feeling.'

'Like a bit of old washing'
Rozanne Hawksley
190 x 190mm (7½ x 7½in)

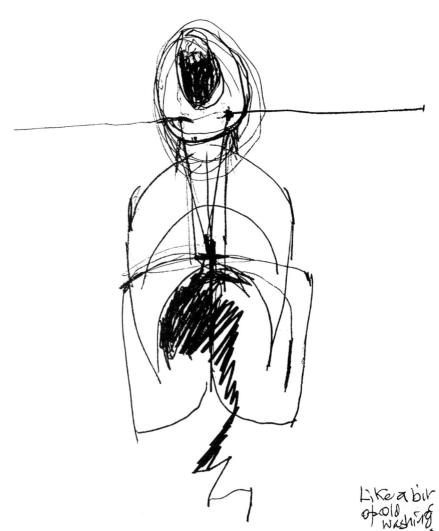

Untitled drawing
Hilary Bower
1999
550 x 550mm (21³/₄ x 21³/₄in)
Gouache on Asian handmade paper, watercolour,
graphite, aquarelle

For some artists, there may be no clear intention when they begin to work in
their sketchbooks. Ideas and developments may flow freely. They may work with
whatever medium comes to hand and the choice of colours may be relatively
spontaneous and expressive rather than representational. This inner world of
memories, fantasies and dreams can be a rich source of inspiration and may also
be a spiritual experience. Drawing partly to find reminders of an experience and
sense of place when she returns home and partly to explore how she thinks and
feels inside, Julia Caprara also seeks a transmission of energy into herself
through working in her sketchbook.

The untitled drawing by Hilary Bower has been completed outside the
sketchbook, but shows a drawing that is deeply contemplative and one that has
been made for personal fulfilment. It is very much a distillation of ideas and
development of personal symbols. Re-creating the idea of 'a sense of place,' it
recalls colours and symbols from a winter visit to Canada (coloured greys, pink
and orange dogwoods), combined with symbols from her local landscape.
Scoring is often used to mark the surface and the seams and stitching, alluding
to walls, are used as compositional devices to section the paper. Part of a series,
this drawing marked a reflective stage between one phase of her work on paper
vessels and later textile developments. As part of a personal dialogue, it
supported contemplation about symbols, emotions and memories.

The way in which your visions and re-visions are communicated is personal
and may differ according to choice or circumstance. Sketchbooks and drawings
can also help to shape a story or narrative. This might be explored through ideas
centred on identity or it may illustrate characters or a plot. Two very different
examples might be the illustrations of Edward Lear compared with those of
Beatrix Potter.

Inventing and designing

Inventing is part of that creative endeavour, along with experimentation, enquiry, research and investigation. A sketchbook provides a space for all kinds of invention and experimentation. This could be with ideas, techniques or media. It could be carried out in a very free way, in which drawings, samples, photographs and notes are all used. On the other hand, it could be a highly structured 'technical' investigation, noting, for example, the steps taken to dye cloth of different fibre types, the quantity of dye, mordant and water needed and the length of time that the fabric has to be in the dye bath. Some textile artists like to formalize these sorts of experiments into a technical file or notebook, which is kept specifically for this purpose. In other cases, the technical experiments and notes may complement freer studies. Consider the difference in keeping this sort of information as represented in my own work on page 88 and that of Dorothy Tucker on page 85. You may prefer to describe this sort of technical experiment as recording or research. The terminology or categorization is not nearly so important as the recording of the practice.

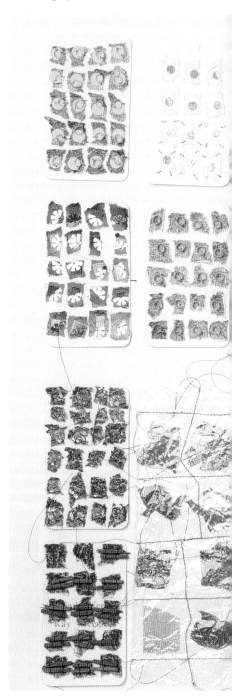

One of the artists featured in this book made the comment that they could not solve design problems without 'making a mark'. In other words, within the design process, drawing is thought translated into action. It might be just a few lines, but its purpose is to capture the essence of an idea. Starting out as jottings, scribbles and rough ideas, the sketches used in the design stage (like the model or maquette stage) may well develop outside the size restrictions of a sketchbook. Stages may be photographed, folded and stored, or kept in a folio and then further re-vision carried out in the sketchbook. This return to the sketchbook to solve visual or technical problems is common to all artists.

Categorizing things is not important, but trying to understand the purposes a sketchbook serves might begin to offer you more freedom with what you do and will boost your confidence in developing a way of approaching thinking, planning and the

Not HV –
belongs to
Stratford – Upon –
Avon College

MAKE YOUR OWN LANTERN PACK

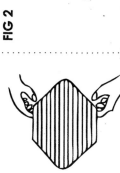

FIG 1

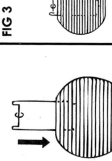

FIG 2

FIG 3

working process. Referring to the practices of other artists and to various different media can be invaluable.

The categories chosen here are intended to prompt further discussion and thought. Whatever purposes your sketchbook serves for you, it is hoped that listing the possibilities might help to focus attention on them, to raise awareness and to give reassurance that what you do has its own place and significance.

Sketchbook: media exploration
Kay Greenlees
A3 (297 x 420mm [11¾ x 16½in])
Papers, plastic, wood, thread, clips, pins

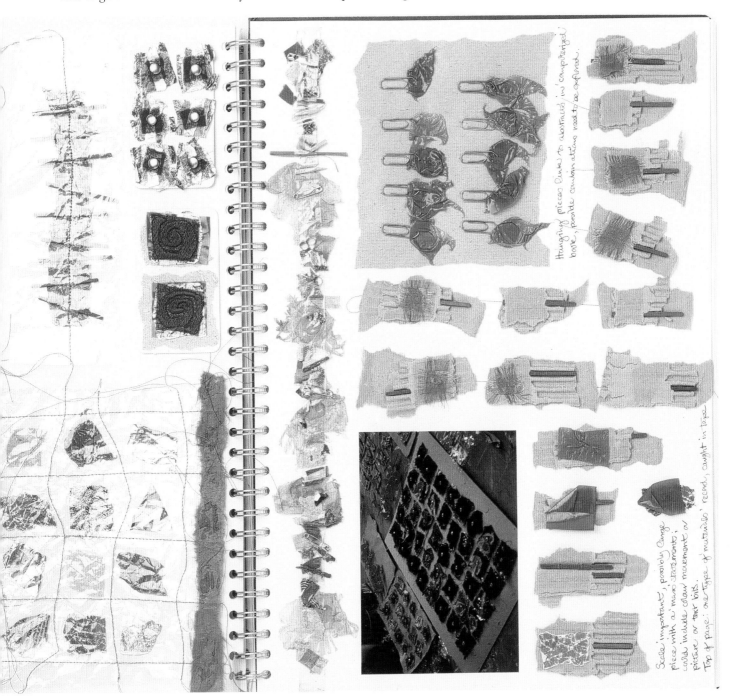

CHAPTER TWO
TEXTILE ARTISTS' WAYS OF SEEING: Different approaches

There is a fundamental paradox in both creating a sketchbook that is personal to you and the expectation that this very personal journey should be shared with others. This tension can be very difficult to resolve. The journey undertaken through working in a sketchbook can be a rocky road. Often, this sharing occurs in a one-to-one situation. In this, we are lucky to enjoy the immense privilege of being able to share the most private work of other people in the most public form of sharing. This brings with it both a degree of responsibility and a trust that should be honoured by all parties.

Once again, I have grouped examples around particular descriptions or approaches, but it would be a mistake to assume that an individual artist worked only in one way, or that his or her work could not be featured under other headings. Where possible, I have tried to show at least two pages of a sketchbook in order to give some flavour of the whole.

There is no intention to show a *process* from the sketchbook leading to resolved pieces of work – that would make this a book about design stages. It would also perpetuate the myth that creative work or thought occurs in a neat, linear progression. Rather, the intention is to show that there are no easy answers. There are no set routes, no step-by-step instructions. A sketchbook is what you make it. You are invited to share the 'visions' and 're-visions' and the various approaches textile artists adopt in their sketchbooks. Aspects of the 'vision' or starting point can be traced in various elements of the sketches or notes. Frequently, the 'vision' is represented by a final piece of work that relates to the sketches but is not a direct translation of them.

Sketchbook: Bali samples *Kay Greenlees*
A4 (210 x 297 mm [8¼ x 11¾ in]) Turban cloth, monoprinting, silk thread

What you see in the sketchbooks is a 'freeze-frame' of the actions *pause, record, reflect, move on...* and the variety of ways that individual textile artists take part in this process.

Sketches prompted by media choices

Often, what marks out textile artists or makers is a delight in handling materials. This delight in both perceived and actual surface qualities is what makes us reach instinctively for a displayed item (despite the notices asking us not to touch the exhibits!). In other words, it is a strong, imperative response that is hard to override. For some makers, their response to their chosen media is very evident in the 'sketchbook' stage of their work; often these books are overflowing and hardly fit between their covers. This is because they use textural materials that express the artists' delight in surface quality. Sometimes, they may have no covers at all as fabric samples are used as a way of sketching. I have chosen to divide artists of this general type into two groups: artists who predominantly work directly in cloth and those who use collage.

Samples as a 'sketching' process

It could be argued that sampling is definitely not sketching. However, I would like to work with a definition of sketching that is sufficiently broad to encompass this stage of textile work. Certainly, sampling conforms to some of the purposes of sketchbook work. It allows the development and exploration of an individual visual language and it supports experimentation with media, albeit in a very focused sense. In particular, sampling sustains the artist's delight in holding and manipulating the cloth. There are two main ways in which sampling is used as part of the sketching process.

Firstly, for many textile artists, producing 'samples' operates as a 'sketch' or preliminary process. Just as some pencil sketches are more developed than others, so too are their fabric equivalents. For some artists, sampling takes the place of drawing on paper and the maker works directly in textile or mixed media. Because cloth has unique qualities that paper doesn't have, some artists are subsequently able to gather their 'sketches' together and form them into larger works. The samples on page 26 were inspired by the colours and patterns of Bali. The shapes and ideas of repetition spring from the temple carvings and the beautiful offerings left there. However, the samples were worked for the sheer enjoyment of exploring the colour, the cloth and the stitch. Although the ideas formed the basis of an experimental textile piece called 'Jewel Book', at the moment these samples are likely to remain in this sketch or trial stage.

Secondly, sampling can be a stage between the initial sketches and the resolved piece. In this case, the samples will be a mixture of aesthetic and more technical experiments, possibly developing notions already explored on paper. These might investigate the contrasts of colour against colour, weight of cloth against weight of thread, size of stitch, matt against shiny, the 'handle' or feel of the materials, the mood they create, how to stiffen a form, how to insert or

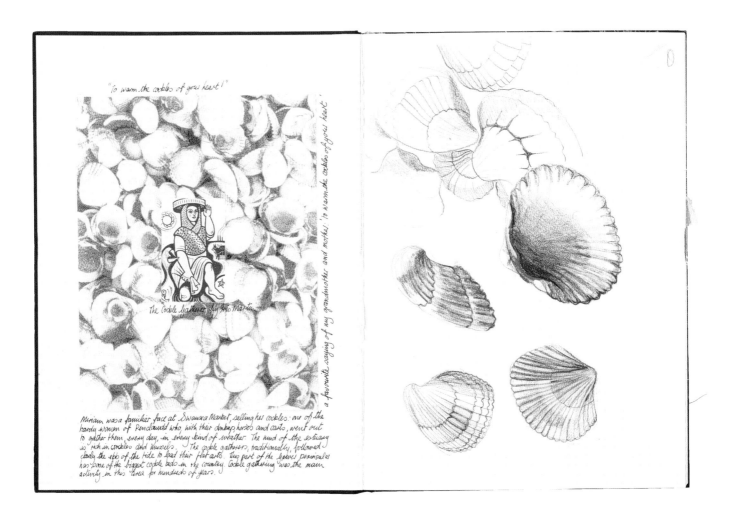

Above:
Cockle sketchbook
Siân Martin
351 x 260mm (14 x 10¼ in)

Left and below:
Cockle (detail)
Siân Martin
380 x 380mm (15 x 15in)
Photography: Siân Martin

fasten wires, how two pieces might join and a range of other options. This is the most common form of sampling, and it augments the work already carried out in the sketchbook. A clear example can be seen in the sketchbook by Siân Martin, seen on page 38. Linking imagery from the work of her mother, Iris Martin, with direct observation, as well as her own Shibori and heat-setting experiments, the samples have become developed enough to be pieces in their own right.

There is no right or wrong way to use samples. Either approach is valid, but I have concentrated on examples of work where samples are a direct recording process in fabric. Sometimes these have been used as a substitute for the paper sketch stage. In these cases, the samples record feelings, thoughts, emotions or ideas that are expressed directly in cloth. Often this way of working is quite intuitive and is also a direct response to the chosen medium – the artist particularly enjoys the feeling of the thread or the fabric in the hand and the way that this can be manipulated to respond to ideas. Fabrics are often collected or hand-dyed to form a large 'palette' of colours from which to select. Particular pieces of work may explore and exploit particular qualities of the fabric, such as softness or transparency. It is common to hear the artist say how much they enjoy the feel of the fabric and this may be a feature of the piece. Often the textile piece(s) are about imaginative, emotive or spiritual concepts, such as joy, vivacity or other moods. Sometimes the response is 'poetic' and lyrical, with fabric elements being made individually and put together to represent a visual event. Like a poem, the piece may be more than the sum of its parts.

The cloth with which she works directly inspires Jenny Bullen. The sketch shown below is worked directly from observation of an old Welsh quilt in an attempt to show the layering and marks worn into the surface. Stitch is used in several ways: as a utilitarian method of joining and layering fabrics, as a mark and as a metaphor.

Sketch
Jenny Bullen
229mm x 178mm (9 x 7in)
Shirting fabric

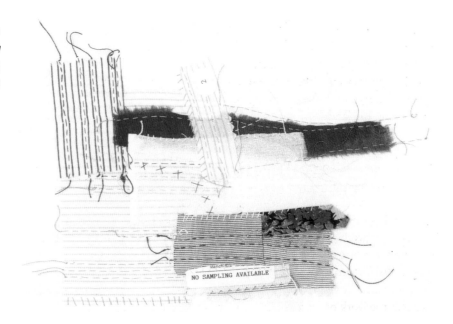

Untitled hanging
Jenny Bullen
2004
635mm x 508mm (25 x 20in)
Hand-dyed lightweight cotton fabrics; silk thread

In the unrelated hanging by the same artist, shown above, the fabric choice and colour palette is entirely different. The fine cotton fabrics have been hand-dyed in indigo and then over-dyed using Procion. Lines have been drawn on this surface with discharge paste and then the fabrics have been layered and stitched through. The colour choice is spontaneous and intuitive and selected because the artist feels that it is right. As the stitch process is lengthy, the artist feels that she needs to be 'at one' or comfortable with the colours while working on them. Stitching occurs intuitively, and the ends of threads for starting and finishing are left as marks on the surface. This strong personal harmony with the colour and stitch is important in meeting the expressive needs of the artist. Worked entirely without reference to paperwork, the hanging is based on ancient field systems and marks in the landscape. Both sketch and hanging record a sustained and developed response to observed surface qualities, with direct analogies traced on the surface of the cloth.

Artists working directly in cloth often use smaller units or pieces of fabric to build larger compositions. Making should always be undertaken as part of the re-vision of a piece, a stage at which creative decisions can still be made. Piecing or assembling the work is part of a very creative process, when a large part of the satisfaction of working is actually holding and stitching the cloth. Stitching as mark-making is usually completed by hand, and the thread selected is equally important to the process in terms of the way it feels, the colour, the weight and the kind of mark it will make. Some of these features, used in different ways, can be seen in the work of Jenny Bullen, Amanda Clayton and Julia Caprara.

Sketchbook pages
Amanda Clayton

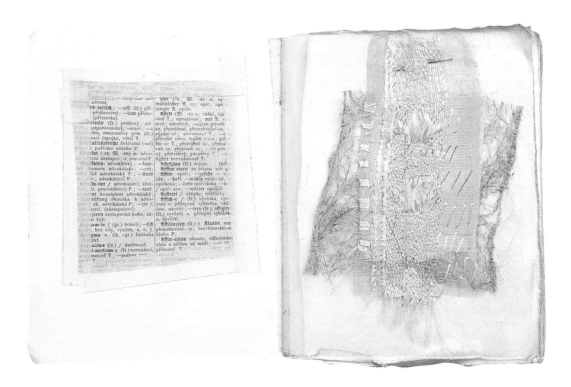

For Amanda Clayton, sampling has become the concept behind her work, as well as her working method. Two examples from her sketchbooks show a delight in the unique characteristics of textile construction and through this the development of a personal artistic language. These pages demonstrate a direct correspondence between the sketchbooks and the textile pieces. Her research also includes an interesting collection of quotations from literature, Victorian domestic advice and recent films. The quotations are themselves direct observations and recordings: like sketches, they take us to the essence of the idea.

> The stitches of those button-holes were so small – so small – they looked as if they had been made by little mice!
>
> From *The Tailor of Gloucester* by Beatrix Potter

The neutral colour palette allows us to focus on the fabric qualities: the marks, shapes, spaces and the weighting of the pieces. The very deliberate, considered composition of each piece seems to belie the self-confessed delight in an intuitive making process and organic construction. However, intuition and insight are often based on a lifetime of experience, here resulting in a care for detail and craftsmanship that again reflects the sampling concept. This is achieved through the emphasis of space and weight as a contrast to the placement of detail, alongside the exploitation of fabric qualities, such as degrees of transparency and opacity. Simple devices, such as counterchange and other uses of positive and negative shapes, have been effectively deployed to achieve emphasis.

These pieces are worked by hand and the enjoyment of the stitch process – holding the needle, working sociably – is particularly important to Amanda Clayton's work, as is the way that the stitch becomes integral to the cloth. First seen in the exhibition 'A Space Odyssey – 2001', the pieces are intended to be viewed in relation to each other. There is a strong impression of 'drawings in space' and the *leitmotif*, sometimes a collar, sometimes a spot, can be seen in context with its boundaries and edges. The work was conceived as a series. Many of the individual elements also explore the idea of sequence, as in the appropriately titled 'Chinese Whispers', in which each collar changes and develops an idea as you move down the panel. The whole set of work coheres around a celebration of sewing and the social history of dress, particularly collars.

Others working directly in cloth will draw and have sketchbooks, but these may be kept in different ways. Sometimes they are a separate activity from the textile work, providing a 'rest' from working with fabric. Occasionally, this kind of book is rather traditional. It is used to record and analyse people, places and things, but there is no attempt to use this process to research for a resolved textile piece, nor will ideas for a textile piece grow from the sketches. Rather, the information gathered in the sketchbook operates to help explore and record composition, colour and mark, only informing the textile resolutions in a very general way.

Using her sketchbooks as a separate activity, but in a way that ultimately relates to her direct work in cloth, Julia Caprara travels her own very individual road. The two sketchbooks featured on page 34 show a direct response to the

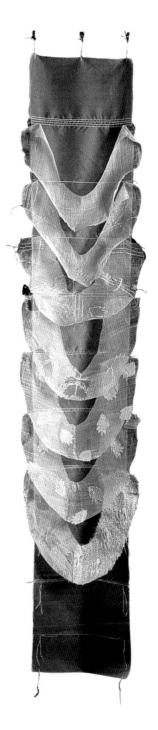

Chinese Whispers
Amanda Clayton
2001
4.6m x 1.82m (15 x 6ft)
Photography: Steve Tanner

Sketchbook: Aegean Sunset
Julia Caprara
A3 (297 x 420mm [11¾ x 16½in])

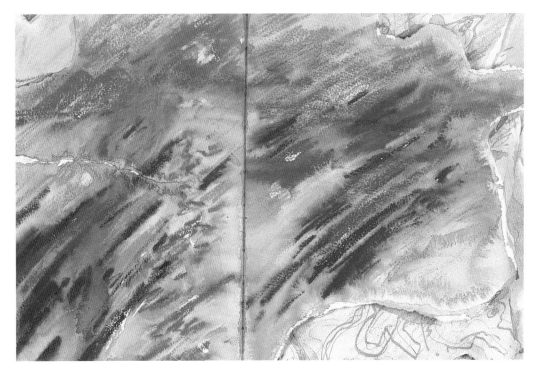

Sketchbook:
Mediterranean Light
Julia Caprara
A3 (297 x 420mm [11¾ x 16½in])

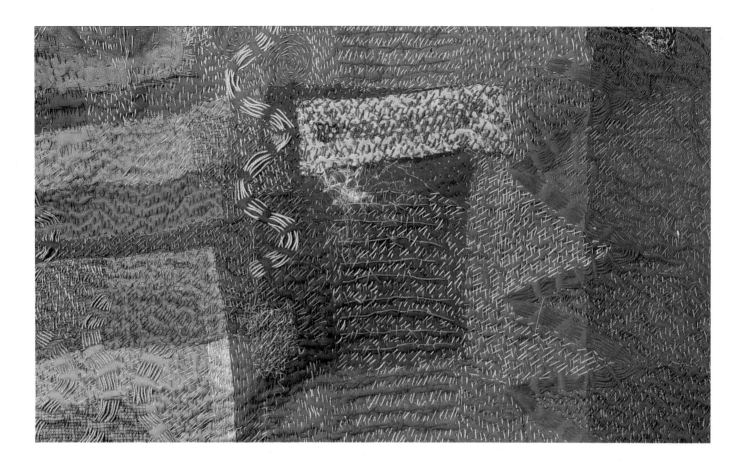

place in which she has chosen to work. Seeking to establish a different sort of 'centre', rather than the literal, she explores the form of the space, or a quality of light and tries to capture the emotional vibration of the place in order to get an individual 'sense of site'. Often, she begins by tearing pages as a way of physically 'earthing' herself into the location. The tears are based on observation: the form of the bay, the sky as a huge arc or the indentations on the surface of the earth. In seeking a sense of mood and vibration, colour may not be real or representative, but chosen to give a sense of heat or light. 'Aegean Sunset' and 'Mediterranean Light' exemplify these points. The detail from 'Kantha for the Family of Man' has colours inspired by the light and energy of the Aegean and Greece. Focused on the Aegean being the heart of the civilized world and the sun being the heart of every person's existence, the quilt acknowledges the necessity for mankind to work together in harmony in order to recognize our true condition. (The Kantha quilts traditionally were gift cloths to celebrate an aspect of human life, such as weddings, birthdays and festivals.)

Whether you use sampling as a sketching process or as an extension of that process, it is important to consider the place that it has in your work. Is it a major vehicle for expression? Is it an 'in between' stage of problem solving and exploration? Or perhaps your ideas blur those boundaries, like the work of Amanda Clayton. However you use sampling, try to understand what it contributes to your personal practice and development.

Kantha for the Family of Man (detail)
Julia Caprara
2 x 10m (78 ¾ x 393 ¾in)
Free-hung wall hanging: layered, hand-stitched textile quilt using running stitch and overlays of applied fabrics and stitching

Helenium Flowers

Ruth Issett

(detail)

Collage

Sketching using collage: texture, pattern and colour

Collage is a technique that excites and appeals to a number of textile artists, possibly because of its very tactile qualities. I have grouped pattern, colour and texture here, because collage is often chosen as the technique most suited to artists exploring these elements of design. Whereas more traditional drawing with pencil, pen or pastel can only create the illusion of surface qualities such as texture and form, collage itself offers the possibilities of actual texture or work in low relief on the page. It is often a method of creating preliminary sketches or studies, because it is seen to be direct and spontaneous. Tearing or cutting papers or fabrics allows for re-positioning and rearrangement before being fixed in place. The method has very obvious limitations for location work, but is useful in the studio or workshop situation, where a wide variety of media is available, messy materials can be coped with easily and space is not at a premium.

Collage is defined as a picture built up wholly or partly from pieces of paper, cloth or other material stuck to a backing. It can be relatively flat, as in collages by the early Cubists, who would stick pieces of newspaper onto pictures otherwise painted in a normal way and by artists such as Matisse, who in his later years used pieces of coloured paper as a complete substitute for painting.

Texture

Collage is essentially an 'additive' process and as such its tactile qualities are exploited by those who enjoy surface texture that can be discerned by touch and by those who enjoy drawing by tearing or cutting shape rather than by using lines. The ability to scrunch, pleat, tear, stitch, fold, punch and generally change the surface of papers before using them to draw or sketch can be exciting, especially when coupled with the opportunity to add a whole range of low-relief items, such as twigs, matches, feathers, wire, lace, keys, coins, cut-out printed images, leaves or other fascinating items.

Many paper types can be used in collage that are unsuitable for sketching in a more traditional way. These range from lightweight papers, such as transparent and tissue papers, Indian and Japanese papers, newspaper, foils and some found papers, to heavier papers, such as envelopes, wrapping papers, corrugated cards and packing papers. Some become firm favourites: for example, brown paper may come to be adopted as a main drawing paper instead of cartridge paper. Many artists favouring collage will alter or manipulate the surface of the paper before beginning work and may keep an extensive collection or palette of 'made' papers for future use. Combined with other techniques, such as printing, foiling, and stitching, the repertoire of materials becomes very personal and quite extensive. (I have used the term 'made' to refer to the customizing of the surface rather than the use of a handmade paper from pulp, although this is also a possibility in your work.)

The sketchbook shown on the opposite page is used in a storage capacity for a selected library of papers made for two different projects. It records the technical processes used to create certain surfaces as well as the sources of the

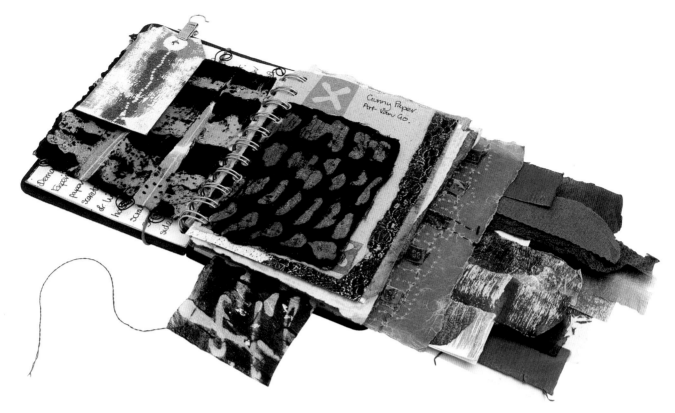

Sketchbook
Kay Greenlees
A6 (105 x 148mm [4¼ x 5¾in])
Various customised papers, wax, graphite, emulsion, wire, plastic, thread

papers. Interesting papers with qualities such as an unusual surface texture or different capacities for absorption can be purchased from specialist suppliers, or equally can be found or recycled, thus keeping the cost of experimentation low. Printed magazine pages can offer a wide range of tonal qualities and can again be very cost-effective, particularly if one recycles magazines that have been used by friends, relations or work colleagues.

Collage can be used for sketching or drawing in a number of ways. As has been pointed out, a collage can be virtually flat, using the shape of the cut or torn paper to describe and analyse form or create pattern. In the case of sketching to achieve form, a clever use of tonal qualities will be more important than textural qualities, although the textural quality may well add to the description or depiction of a particular surface. If it is reasonably flat, then collage can also be drawn on or into. Both the ability to depict form and a delight in the surface quality can be seen in the drawing of a Savoy cabbage by Emma Winstanley (below).

Savoy Cabbage
Emma Winstanley
A1 (594 x 891mm [23¼ x 35in])
Mixed media: papers, fabrics, inks

Sketchbook pages
Siân Martin
2004
350 x 260mm
(13¼ x 10¼in)
Pen, wax, ink
drawings,
photographs

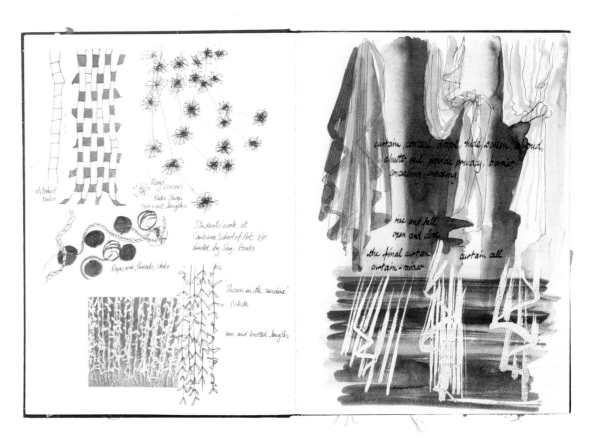

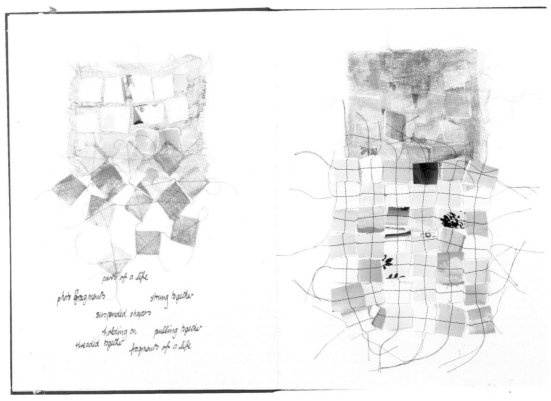

Often collage work develops into an exuberant celebration of colour and textural qualities. It may appeal to those with a love of collecting and with an acquisitive instinct for the small treasures and *objets trouvés* that find their way onto the surface of the work. Adding found items, magazine pictures or photographs can provide a narrative for the piece. Utilizing some of the techniques mentioned in this section, and crossing some of the boundaries used to describe work here, I have included some sketchbook pages by Siân Martin, which show how she has brought some of these ideas together, resulting in a unique hanging. *How Green Was My Valley* is one of several 'curtain' forms developed in relation to family memories. These include torn fragments of photographs, dyed and printed fabrics, curtain studies and various pieces of inspiration from her visits to Japan and Australia.

Above:
How Green Was My Valley (detail)
Siân Martin
Hanging 100 x 60cm (39 x 23¼in)
Mixed media

Left:
How Green Was My Valley
Siân Martin
Hanging 100 x 60cm (39 x 23¼in)
Mixed media

Pattern

Pattern involves the repetition of related or similar shapes within a composition. It is usually associated with decorative surfaces, although it can apply equally to picture-making, and both aspects are relevant to embroiderers. Pattern need not employ regularity and it can be asymmetrical as well as symmetrical. There are several different examples throughout the book, the most obvious being on pages 10, 26, 33, 35 and 117. You will be able to see many more yourself. Elements of pattern can also be used in construction and three-dimensional work.

In the sketchbook pages by Jan Evans, collage and pattern come together in her explorations of Fijian bark cloth, in which she enjoys working with a palette of prepared papers as well as charcoal, pastel and frottage. The sewing machine has been used as a drawing implement to develop the geometric pattern, and her textile working methods tend to echo those of the sketches.

A feature of both Fijian and African bark cloth is that local pigments have been used for colouration. Inspired by this idea, Jan used locally mined ochre from the Clearwell Caves in the Forest of Dean, England, to develop her subtle colour palette. There are four different kinds used in her work and as pigments they need the 'body' or support of gesso, acrylic gel or emulsion. In her studio development work on the opposite page, Jan has developed the pattern theme from the bark cloth by combining it with her studies of local landscapes, where the abstraction of the pine trees on the skyline echoes the abstract form seen in the other sketches. They are based on the idea of landscape and legend, with the colours relating to the subtlety of snowy British winters.

Sketchbook
Jan Evans
A3 (297mm x 420 mm [11¾ x 16½ in])
2004
Pattern: observed bracken frond, pen, waxed photographs, bonding, machine stitching

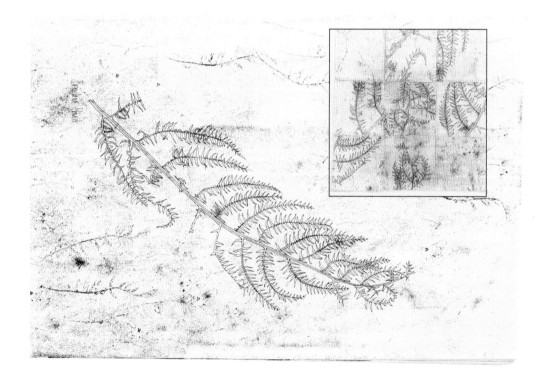

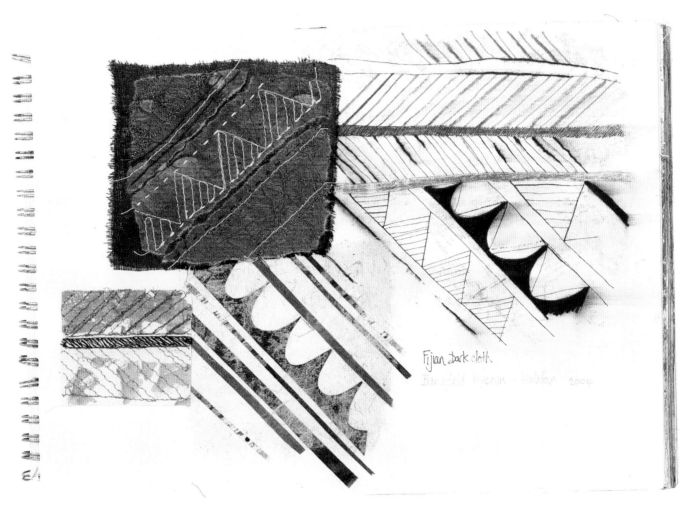

Fijian Dark cloth.
Bankfield Museum - Halifax 2004

Sketchbook
Jan Evans
A4 (210 x 297mm [8¼ x 11¾ in])
2004
Natural ochres, charcoal, pen, papers,
fabrics, machine stitch

Studio work 2004
Jan Evans
Pattern: ideas developed from the landscape and
legend series

Colour

Colour can, of course, be used in the sketching process in any way that one wishes. Colour used on location is necessarily limited, as discussed on page 72. Suggestions for using coloured pages to support your sketching can be found on page 118.

The sketch examples chosen here look at colour as a main source of inspiration and investigation. Colour can be one of the most difficult concepts to use. Many artists work totally intuitively, while others deliberately explore the associated concepts in order to better understand their own practices and to be able to control and use these to greater effect.

Collage may offer a good way of exploring or learning about the interaction between colours. Another approach may be to use collage materials in only one colour – for example, bringing together a range of different reds. Exploring the different qualities within a colour would be worthwhile: the warmth of orange-reds, for example, against the cooler mauve-reds; the reds that 'sing out' because of the intensity and saturation of the pigment as opposed to a softer, watery red. It is clearly possible to explore colour through techniques other than collage. Dyeing and painting, printing and stitch all offer exciting and quite different challenges.

Ruth Issett is well known for her use of vibrant and intense colour, both on paper and fabric. Her technical knowledge is prodigious and well documented in her publications. This lifetime of experience in mixing colours clearly informs her intuitive choices when working. Her fabric and paper works always reflect the pleasure that she feels in creating with colour. It is a constant voyage of discovery that permeates all she does. Colour itself is the vehicle or concept that she explores. In the samples and sketches seen here, she has explored two different starting points that are beginning to be brought together for her latest

Above: Winter colour stitch sample
Ruth Issett
300 x 150mm (12 x 6in)
Hand-dyed fabrics and stitch: direct observation of winter dogwood

Right: Colour studies on paper
Ruth Issett
480 x 650mm (19 x 26in)
Colour studies developed from the stitch sample

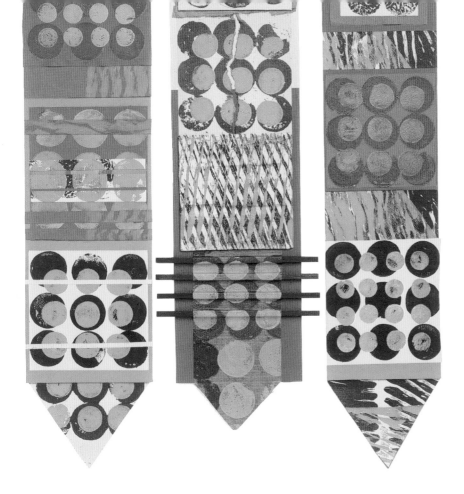

piece of work. Direct observation of winter colour, the orange-coloured stems of the dogwoods and willows against yellow fir trees and a bright sky have inspired the stitch sample (above left). In its turn this has been the starting point for the colour in the larger scale paper sketches (below left). Finally, the samples (above) take their colour and pattern inspiration from an 18th century Chinese skirt. The combination of the shape and form has inspired the title 'Whirling Dervish' and provides the subject for her latest textile hanging.

The language used to describe colour is often thought difficult and may be off-putting. Some may be inspired by this technical challenge to extend the boundaries and the potential of the medium that they have chosen to use. Not all media respond in the same way, or will result in the same colours when they are mixed. This is particularly important for textile artists, as pigments, dyes and coloured light (as on the computer) will respond in different ways and require specific experimentation. It is commonly thought that all other colours can be mixed from the primary colours, red, blue and yellow. 'Secondary' colours are those made by combining two primary colours, resulting in orange, green and purple. This is generally truer for pigment (as in paint), although it is difficult to achieve certain colours because some pigments are not absolutely pure. Other terms that may be useful are:

- Hue or purity
- Chroma or intensity or brightness
- Tone or value – lightness or darkness
- Tertiary colours
- Complementary colour
- Tints and shades
- Discord and harmony

Colour and pattern studies
Ruth Issett
490 x 350mm (19¼ x 14in)
Inspired by an 18th-century skirt

- Colour perception
- Local colour
- Reflected colour

The bibliography and reading lists at the end of the book will serve as an indication of those texts that may be useful in exploring these areas further. If terminology appears confusing or contradictory, it is worth checking the origin of the publication. British, American or European authors may be drawing on specific scientific and cultural theories about colour, resulting in slight but confusing differences in definition.

The history of colour production is fascinating. For the most part, early pigments came from clays or minerals: for example, yellow ochre and brown umber, with ultramarine being made from the semi-precious stone lapis lazuli. Textile colours that penetrated the fibres tended to come from the plant world. Flowers, leaves, mosses, roots and lichens all yielded colour. Purple and carmine came from the animal world. The ancient 'silk routes' and subsequent trade links exploited by the British and Dutch East India companies dealt in these rare and precious items. Colour also has a fascinating history, with different cultures perceiving and using colour in their own ways. As well as aesthetic qualities, colour is often imbued with magical and symbolic meanings and ceremonial status or significance. There has also been much research into the psychology and science of colour; how it makes us feel, how it can affect mood as well as to give warning and direct social behaviour patterns. Since we read colour faster than letters or numbers, it can be our most immediate perception. Whole sketchbooks, notebooks or research journals could be kept to explore the areas mentioned above.

Models and maquettes as a sketching process

Many artists use textiles or textile processes as part of their work in three dimensions, or work in relief. The sketching stage(s) of the work will not necessarily differ from other sketching processes but, as with other more tactile approaches, the work will move into three-dimensional explorations that involve samples, maquettes and models as part of the development work. This will be seen as vital to the resolution of the work and it is unlikely that a drawing or sketch will be transcribed literally, as it would leave little room for creative development in the making. This creative development could include extensive work in the maquette stage in which mass, weight, volume, balance, scale and form begin to relate to material and viewpoint as the outcome develops.

Broadly based three-dimensional experiments will gradually pave the way for more focused development as the initial research informs new and innovative designs that take on a life of their own. Much of this process – problem-finding and problem-solving – has to be carried out 'in the round' and will not be in sketchbook form. The sketchbook may only be used for initial research and

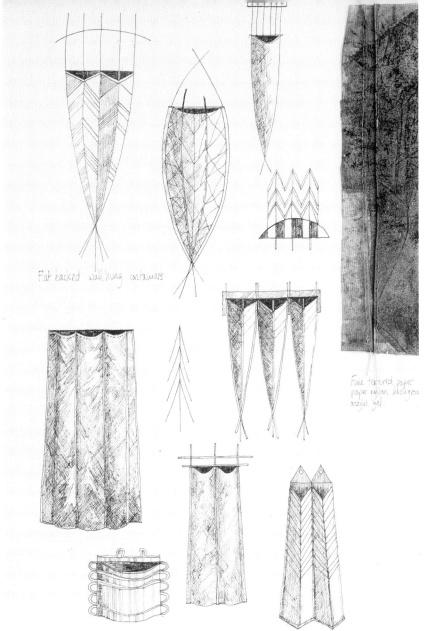

Flat backed wall hung containers

Fine textured paper
paper nylon bichigrou
acrylic gel.

Sketchbook page: wall-hung vessels
Jan Evans
A3 (297mm x 420mm [11¾ x 16½in])

analysis and then perhaps to record the making process. This could be in the form of samples, photography, drawings, notes and materials exploration – whatever is needed to support the ideas. It may include suppliers, contractors and other professional contacts. A more useful description in this instance might be workbook or log, rather than sketchbook.

Three-dimensional work in textiles can be quite a broad area, encompassing jewellery, sculpture, installation, products, interior design and 'vessels'. When considering three-dimensional objects, the relationship between form and function should be considered carefully. A form or volume has three dimensions – height, width and depth (or thickness) – whether it is solid mass or hollow. Freestanding forms can be made from card or paper. Design solutions may include compromise. Sculpture may concentrate on form. Its function is not best described in utilitarian but in visual or aesthetic terms. Its function, in effect, is as a direct appeal to our emotions. Through this we share the artist's experiences. 'Vessels', although popular in textiles, cannot function in the way that ceramic or wooden ones do, and it is arguable that their function could be purely visual, decorative or emotional. Sketches for wall-hung vessels can be seen above.

Part of the sketch or model stage may help resolve possible questions of function, such as, 'does a three-dimensional work of art/textile have to have a function?' Or maybe, 'should the personal satisfaction of the artist be enough?' Some of the functions that a work of art/textile might have are:

• To decorate
• To inform
• To commemorate, a person or event
• To make feelings or emotions come alive
• To communicate or form part of a dialogue

How will these functions affect the form of the work?

Sketching or drawing of form

If this is your preferred way of working, it is likely that you have already explored the most suitable ways of drawing to link to your three-dimensional models. There is a wealth of published material by several 20th-century sculptors that illustrate how they recorded form. The drawings of Henry Moore are particularly accessible and show a variety of methods that may be helpful, ranging from wax resist and wash, gouache or crayon to even the humble biro.

What characterizes the drawings or sketches for three-dimensional work is that they explore the possibilities of the form of an object. Sometimes the sketches show this from many different angles, as though one were walking around the object. If you haven't got a personal starting point, there are several common ways to practise drawing form that might be helpful. Albrecht Dürer drew everyday domestic items, such as pillows, using directional line to indicate form. Examples of draped forms can be seen in the drawings of Raphael, Leonardo and Michelangelo. Simple starting points might be screwed-up paper, knotted fabric or other highly textured surfaces, all of which are ideal, especially if lit well. Wrapped forms can also be tried.

Hidden forms can heighten other senses and provide a challenge in drawing forms that have been perceived by touch rather than sight.

1. Prepare several lightweight calico bags of a suitable size. (Pillowcases are fine).
2. Put an object, either a natural or manmade form, inside a bag. (It works best if you don't know what the object is, so enlist the help of family or friends, or prepare the exercise a few weeks in advance and come back to it when you have forgotten what you put in each bag. Alternatively, work in a group and swap bags.) Tie the top with a thread or ribbon or secure with clothes pegs.
3. Carefully feel the form through the bag – try not to decide what it is.
4. Draw what you feel, taking care to describe from touch, the surface, the shape and the proportions. Annotate to help establish what the object feels like. Does it feel heavy? Can you feel joins, flaps, edges, hollows and so on? The drawings could be several small studies of different parts of the object, or the whole piece.
5. Next, take the object from the bag and draw it from several viewpoints, maybe changing media as required.

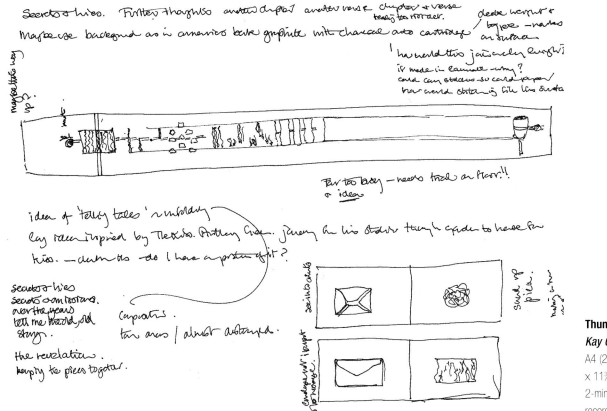

Thumbnail sketches
Kay Greenlees
A4 (210 x 297mm (8¼ x 11¾in)
2-minute jottings to record an idea

Natural form

Choose a natural object, such as a flower head, shaped pebble, bone or shell, that can be drawn from several different viewpoints. (The poppy head by Rose Horspool on page 21 is an example.)

Make a series of studies until you feel that you understand the object. These studies might provide the raw material for constructing a maquette, which could be made of card, wire, wood or a more malleable material, such as Plasticine, clay or fabric. You can experiment by combining different views that you have studied in one form. Will the form be free-standing (on the floor or hanging from the ceiling) or 'in relief'?

Models

Often, three-dimensional work will require the solution to complex problems, explored through the process of sketching and making maquettes. These small-scale models show what the finished form will look like. They are used to sort out technical problems of structure and balance. They can be used to explore what the object will look like from different angles. Once made, the maquettes themselves may be the subject of exploration by sketching and re-making, so that this stage becomes dynamic and creative. Solving the technical problems may require drawings that are more akin to diagrams or maps, as well as practical experiments that show how things join, articulate or move.

Often the maquette or model stage of the work isn't saved or recorded by the artist. In the case of an ordinary practising artist, this will probably be due to lack of storage space. While perfectly understandable, this certainly highlights the importance for students of recording this part of their 'sketching' or preliminary work. Visits to Henry Moore's studio in Hertfordshire, or Barbara Hepworth's studios in Cornwall, show whole collections of models and maquettes. In common with Moore, many artists commission others to do their making or construction, and the maquette is the object that contains the information that the maker will need. In this, the maquette functions in a similar way to a toile in the fashion industry.

Research for my piece 'Underrated Treasures' contains a model stage that functioned in a similar way to a toile. Several of the sketchbook stages can be seen opposite. Some 'thumbnails', from 2002, record the earliest stages of the idea to incorporate cloth and sewing machine together. In collating research for an exhibition at the Bankfield Museum, Halifax, some two years later, the idea began to take form. The sketchbook stages here show my recordings of a 'sense of place' as I move from gallery to gallery, trying to see it with fresh eyes. The inserts between the pages note my major concerns. These included paintings of women involved in textile work, sketches and photographs of Edwardian costume, and an outline drawing of a small sewing machine. The half page of suffragette colours carries the summary of my interests. There are another two pages of this type.

Below: **Underrated Treasures**
Kay Greenlees
Height 144cm (56in)
2004
Photography: Jerry Hardman-Jones

Above: **Sketchbook page: Underrated Treasures** *Kay Greenlees*

A3 (297 x 420mm [11¾ x 16½in]) 2004 Creating a sense of place and identifying themes Photography: Jerry Hardman-Jones

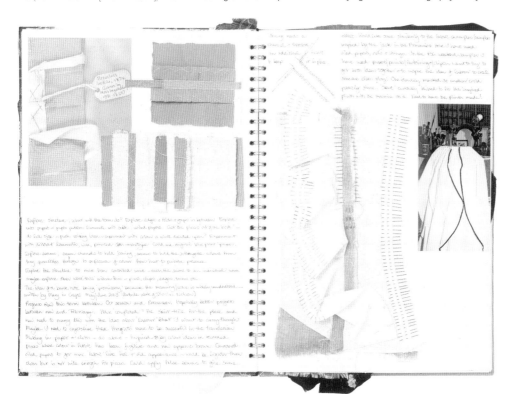

Left: **Sketchbook page: Underrated Treasures**

Kay Greenlees

A3 (297 x 420mm [11¾ x 16½in])

2004

Developing the model: toile stage

The interests drawn from these pages include:

• The dichotomy inherent in the picture of the working girls in the Charles Horner workrooms – their drab costume against the fabulous jewels
• The 'hidden' suffragette statement, in the costume gallery (the fabric carried suffragette colours in the selvedge, inside the garment)
• The sewing machines – displayed as inventions

I focused on ideas concerning the identity of the female workers in comparison to the identity of the female consumers of either the jewellery or the costumes. The sewing machine, which was exhibited as 'an invention', was removed from its context as an item within either a commercial or domestic workroom. In exploring the increasingly dynamic identity of 'the working girl' in Edwardian times, the piece makes construction explicit, using it to suggest visible adornment, and relocates the sewing machine as part of the process by which women variously formed identities. The very necessary pins have been moved to the outside to function as jewels or treasure and their quantity and repetition suggest the labour involved in women's work. Both the needlework tools and the women are implied in the title 'Underrated Treasures'. The second sketchbook stage, at the bottom of page 49, shows the model or toile being constructed to determine the form of the work, together with several of the fabric samples, as a consideration of edge finishes.

Joining materials *Kay Greenlees*
A2 (590 x 420mm [23¼ x 16½in])

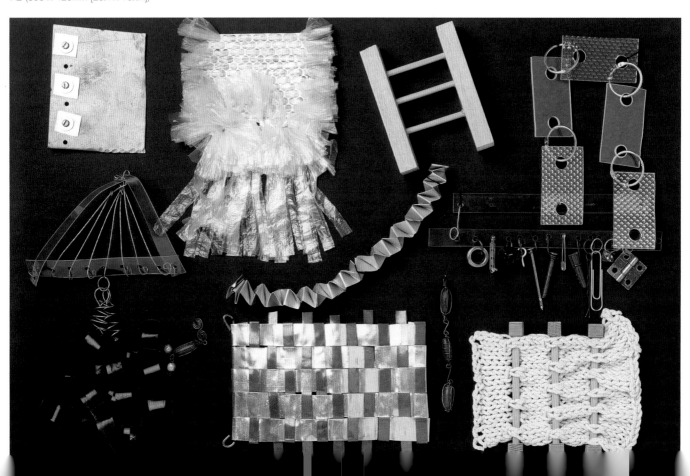

Beginning to work in relief

Experiments in joining materials can be very useful and creative. Try joining:

- Fabric to wood
- Wood to metal
- Metal to fabric
- Fabric to plastic

The object would be to find as many creative ways of doing this as possible. Many of these suggestions may be too bulky or too large to be stored in a sketchbook, so you may need to draw and photograph these stages to ensure that they are kept for future reference. Examples can be seen on the opposite page.

Paper is one of the least expensive and yet most versatile materials for three-dimensional experimentation. With all of the suggestions below, it is advisable to keep to white paper so that form is paramount.

- Try to find as many ways as possible of joining paper to paper – without adhesive or fasteners!
- Find as many ways as possible of altering the surface of paper – crease, bend, tear, roll, pleat, punch. Mount and present these. Light the samples in different ways to explore the relief qualities of the surface.
- Make a variety of forms, such as tubes, or use ready-made tubes. Arrange and develop these considering size, weight, scale, proportion and balance. Use different methods of joining each group: cocktail sticks, giant paper clips. How do these alter the nature of the assemblage?
- Work with multiples: add individual units to each other to build a form. Experiment with size and scale. Light and then draw this form, or interesting parts of it.

Above: **Crumpled paper**

Left: **Paper curls**

A development of the last suggestion can be seen in the simple forms below. 'Made' or customized papers have been used. The 'base' paper has been repeated as a common element in each form. Each multiple becomes more complex but remains related to the previous one, and the method of fastening has been allowed to become increasingly prominent until it is a fully decorative element. Colour has been kept to a minimum, but has been added in thread and fabric, also increasing as the form develops.

In relief: Multiple forms
Kay Greenlees
260 x 260mm (10¼ x 10¼in)

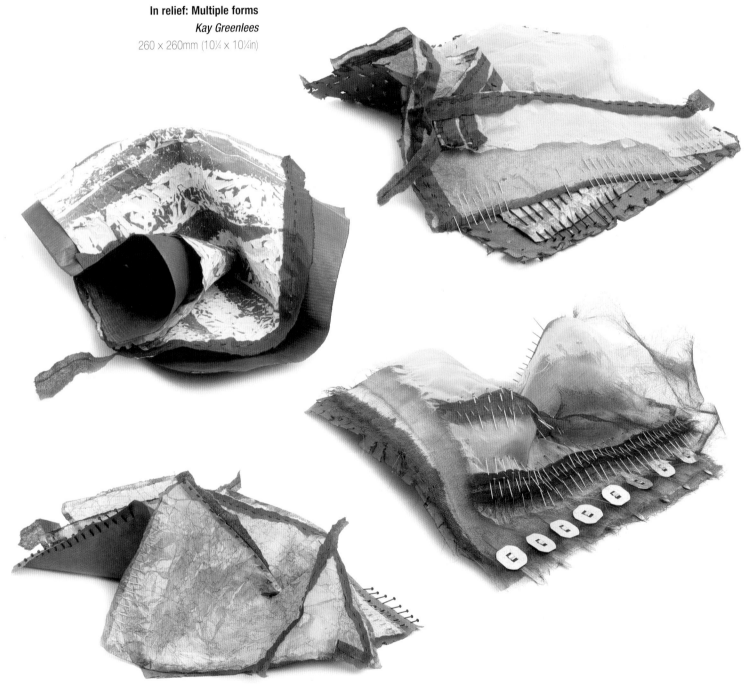

Left:
Monday's Child is Fair of Face
Linda Livesey
Length 60cm (24in)
Silk, wire, beads
Photography: Linda Livesey

Collage

Try using bulky, non-textile items to form a collage. Select materials that have different textures and contrasts: off-cuts of wood, coarse fabric, wires, wire mesh, corrugated card, sheet metal, bubble wrap, natural wood, twigs. Reproduce a section of one of your drawings of form using this method. This may provide a halfway house between the sketching stage and beginning to work in three dimensions. Several drawings and developments might be suggested.

Form

Experiment, too, with different kinds of form:

- Organic forms – reflect those usually found in nature
- Open forms – bowl, plate or dish-type forms
- Closed forms – bottles or flasks
- Fun forms – often the form is in direct contradiction to the function of the object, such as a Mickey Mouse phone
- Abstract forms – often hard-edged forms in space
- Figurative and/or narrative forms
- Divisional forms – screens

Research the kind(s) of forms that interest you or that offer most potential for the development of your ideas. Open forms or those with a large surface area, such as divisional forms (screen shapes, for example), may offer the most potential for decorative surfaces. Decoration should always complement the form and may be most effective when understated.

Linda Livesey finds an interesting combination of ideas based on form in her series of 'dresses'. Developed from her cacti studies (see page 10 and 11), these incorporate spiky surface textures in combination with a dress form. Each about 60cm (24in) long, they depict the days of the week in the children's verse 'Mondays child is fair of face…'. Although the cacti provide a rich source of inspiration, especially through the repetition and textures of their surfaces, the dress surfaces evolve as she works on them.

Section of a drawing 'in relief'
Kay Greenlees
460 x 130mm (18 x 5¼in)

In the form by Sarah Burgess below, the surface quality is an integral part of the work and colour is used as an expressive element. Completed as a set of four – 'Tear', 'Split', 'Capture', and 'Held' – these forms explore the idea of wrenching apart; a cold, hard exterior against a burning interior. Stable forms are being pulled towards instability.

Decoration on form doesn't always have to be added. It may be taken away by cutting into the surface. If your form is decorated, then this will need the same sketchbook exploration as other areas of the work. Is it to scale? How will the scale affect the working method? Is the decoration integral to the form? Exploration of forms from other cultures will often reveal interesting combinations of line, pattern, colour and texture. These reveal how many of the elements can be combined before the function of the object becomes disguised. Decoration is most often effective when balanced with plain areas to allow the eye to rest and to appreciate the form.

In the work by Sarah Burgess on page 55, the sketchbook explores and records the already made maquettes and their relationship to one another. The sketch is made in order to develop the idea and to reflect on the piece. For this artist, drawing is seen as vital to the revision of the idea; thinking and drawing are synonymous. Without paper and mark-making, there isn't any design development; making a mark and reacting to it is how the process comes into being. The ideas relate to others inspired by architecture, columns and space. The annotations hint at some of the issues important to the artist: spaces in between the forms; the use of darkness and light to suggest meaning, atmosphere and emotion, and the difference between looking in and looking out. Almost the whole sketchbook explores these preoccupations. Rhythm becomes important in some sketches, surface and materials in others. This page (and many others) shows an interesting combination of closed forms and divisional forms. Final developments from these ideas can be seen in the image 'Connected' on the opposite page. This three-dimensional form explores positive and negative space and the contradictions of solidity and fragility.

Split *Sarah Burgess*
250 x 400 x 80mm (9¾ x 15¾ x 3¼ in)
Surface: graphite and rust-treated material, acrylic paint, light-gathering plastic and stitch
Photography: Sarah Burgess

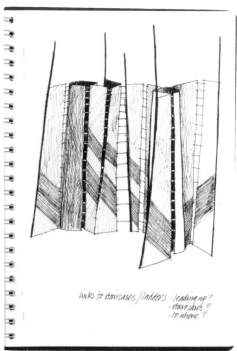

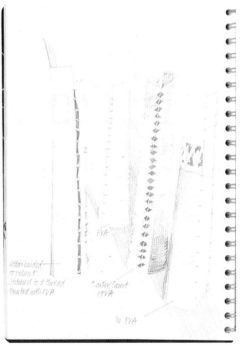

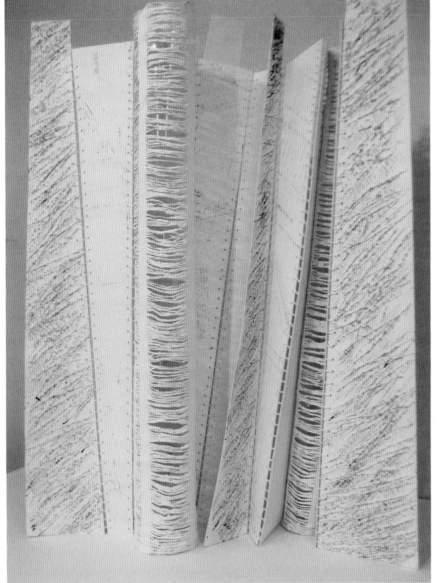

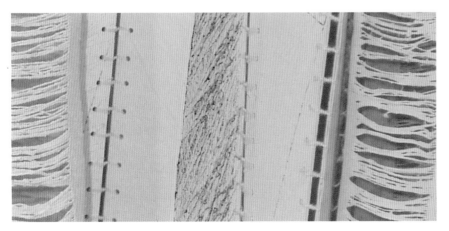

Above: **Sketchbook pages: Development sketches for Connected**
Sarah Burgess
A4 (210 x 297mm [8¹/₄ x 11³/₄in])

Top left: **Connected** *Sarah Burgess*
70 x 76 x 35cm (27¹/₂ x 30 x 13³/₄in) 2002
Drawn-thread towers connected by knotted stitch to mixed-media panels stitched and printed with architectural drawings

Left: **Connected (detail)** *Sarah Burgess*

Sketch of Sailor
Rozanne Hawksley

The final sketchbook pages in this section are by Rozanne Hawksley. They show some of the research she conducted at the Naval Dockyard and Museum in Portsmouth, the Wellcome Institute of Medicine and the National Maritime Museum. 'For Alice Hunter…' is a tribute to her grandmother, who sewed sailors' collars. The subject matter touches concerns that are common to many of Rozanne Hawksley's pieces: the immorality and pitiable nature of war and the frailty of the human condition. The work is presented as an assemblage of objects, utilizing both wall and floor space, that are a visualization of a journey of stitches, from the making of the collar to the wounded sailor, through to his burial at sea. What we can see here is research for the middle of the narrative: the wounded sailor. The sketches illustrate two aspects of this. Firstly, this shows the way that the metal plate was fixed to the skull and the implements that were needed for this task. Secondly, the original sketches for the sutures that the surgeon would have used to close the wound. In both cases, the visualization is completed by showing the finished presentation from within the group, with the skull presented on the

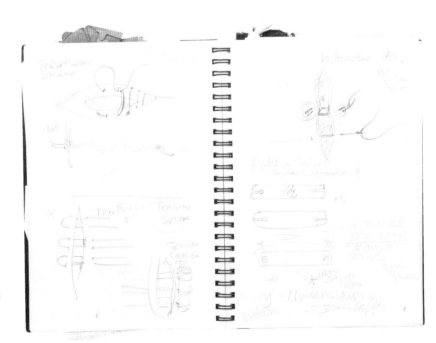

Sketchbook pages
Rozanne Hawksley
A5 (148mm x 210mm [5¾ in x 8¼ in])
Recording the surgeon's stitches

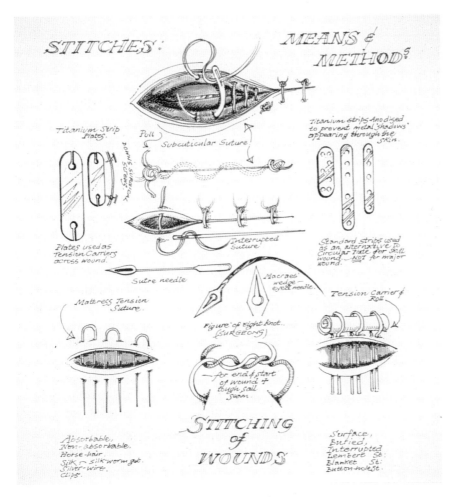

For Alice Hunter…
Rozanne Hawksley
Presented surgeon's sutures

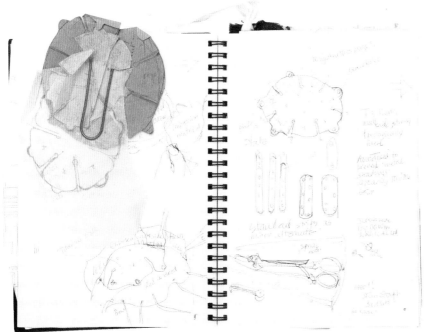

Sketchbook pages
Rozanne Hawksley
A5 (148mm x 210mm [5¾ in x 8¼ in])
Recording the skull plate shape and fastenings

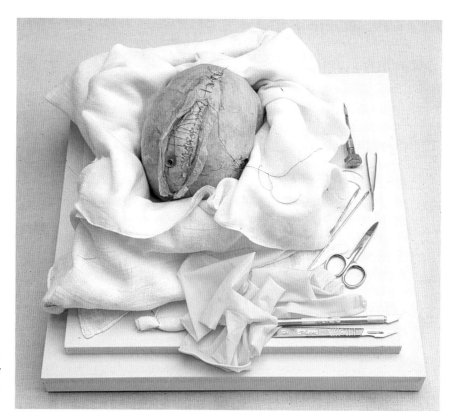

For Alice Hunter...
Rozanne Hawksley
Presented skull injury

floor and the diagrammatic sutures on the wall. The sketch for the sailor is shown alongside the floor-mounted piece for the collar. Other pages in the sketchbook show elaborate and thorough calculations for the coffin and the poles for carrying it, investigations for the making of the collar, materials for these ideas, contacts, reading, the routes and delivery of the cloth and notes for the blacksmith. The ideas for presenting the work are generally given in words rather than as three-dimensional sketches.

For Alice Hunter...
Rozanne Hawksley
Presented collar

Sketchbook approaches to conceptual pieces

The work of some artists is not necessarily inspired by visual starting points, but by what I have termed a concept or idea. The inspiration for making a visual statement may be personal, political, social, environmental or cultural. This is developed as a response to the way the artist feels about a certain issue. Although it's likely that they will make the piece to explore the issue for their own interest, the intention may also be to engage the audience with its meaning(s). What the work is *about* is much more important than what it is *of*.

Conceptual works may be more difficult to 'read' or understand when viewed in an exhibition, and may raise more questions than they answer. In this sense, it's nearly always easier to look at a piece inspired by the landscape or pattern, where the starting point is evident, and the stages involved in production are more easily understood. Equally, the subject matter for conceptual pieces may be demanding or contentious, or contain emotional qualities from which an audience may want to walk away. Some audiences, artists or makers don't want the additional challenge of wondering precisely what the work is about; others are not happy until they have wrestled with the issue. Often, artists will explore their theme through many pieces and will return to it again and again throughout their working lives, as they find new things to 'say' about the issue. The work may, therefore, be part of an ongoing internal dialogue, or one that involves an audience. Some conceptual pieces may offer clues to the meaning(s) of the work; often the title will provide a starting point, as may figurative qualities or implied narrative.

Sketchbook page
Jan Miller
A4 (210 x 297mm [8¼ in x 11¾ in])
Costume sketch using paper and stitch
as textile analogy

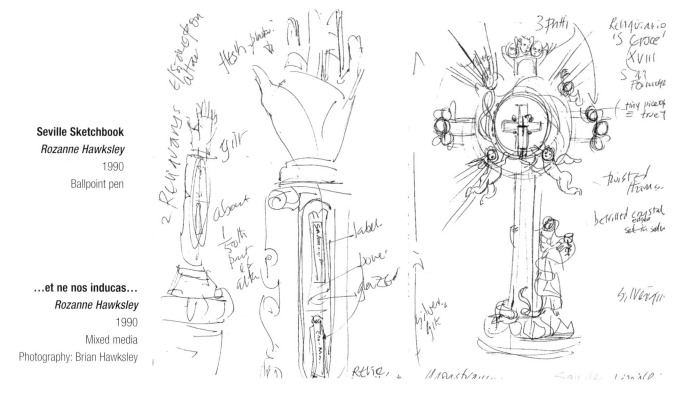

Seville Sketchbook
Rozanne Hawksley
1990
Ballpoint pen

…et ne nos inducas…
Rozanne Hawksley
1990
Mixed media
Photography: Brian Hawksley

What sort of sketchbook work is behind some of the pieces that I have selected for this section of the book? If the starting point for the idea behind the work is not initially visual (as in, say, colour, pattern or natural forms), then what use do the artists make of the sketchbook or sketchbook stage of their work? If they draw, what purpose(s) does this serve? How do they make visual the ostensibly non-visual concept of their starting point? Perhaps the piece is visualized or seen 'in the mind's eye' and then aspects of it are researched as necessary. What sort of relationship exists between the sketch or notebook stage and the resolved textile piece?

Rozanne Hawksley provides us with a clear example of work that involves an ongoing internal dialogue, and one with an audience. In an article for *The World of Embroidery* in 1997 she says, 'I am attempting to deal with themes of isolation and suffering due to war, sickness, poverty, death, and increasingly, the misuse of power'. These serious and difficult issues are not immediately visual, although some have obvious associated symbolism.

The sketchbook page above shows quick, dynamic drawings and annotations that clearly communicate those objects and ideas that most fascinated the artist at the time. Sketched in Seville during Holy Week, and in a great hurry due to circumstance, they are reminders, possibly to be used later to add to collected emotional and visual mind-stored references. The annotations reveal an interest in reliquaries and things associated with them: labels, bone, glazing, silver gilt, and bevelled crystal edges. The size and positioning of these beside the cross on the altar is also noted. These sketches are different in kind from those drawings of herself, such as 'In Grief' pictured opposite and 'Like a Bit of Old Washing' on page 22. The Seville sketches were made for a different purpose and contain little or no feeling. Despite a clear congruence between the Seville and Granada sketches and a resolved piece such as '…et ne nos inducas…' ('…and lead us not…') the actual way that thought is externalized is not explicit, even to the artist. The form of the work 'comes as a matter of a hidden agenda, the centre of feeling dictating a visual form, …followed by some really hard thinking and the

decision of 'how?', and 'with what?' which leads to the use of only those materials and no others, that are absolutely necessary to the thinking.' Here the sketches and the resolution of the work happened alongside each other. In its enclosure '…*et ne nos inducas…*' hints at the secret, the personal and the intimate; symbolism and allegory are used alongside the ornate opulence that is redolent of the Catholic Church.

By contrast, the drawing 'In Grief' is an entirely emotional response to the death of her son. The expression of the same feeling is articulated in 'I will fly south to the sun and the sea, now my Time has come' – for Matthew 8.1.95. This moving and beautiful *in memoriam* captures the frailty of the human condition as some of the fine threads that tether the bird to the earth are broken and it begins to rise towards a golden and altogether different plane of existence.

Both of these pieces show an interrelationship between 'the sketch' and a resolution that does not conform to the idea of a neat 'step-by-step' process, but rather demonstrates a very real dynamic between these two areas of work that make them interdependent.

Conceptual pieces may be less likely to be made only in textile or thread and are rather more likely to include mixed media. This is because the media will be selected that best suits the expression or exploration of the idea behind the work (as in the mixed-media pieces discussed above.) So it might be that textile artists move away from using textiles on some occasions, just as other artists utilize textiles when the need arises and what they want to say is best expressed by the use of thread or cloth. An example of this would be 'Love Poem' (1996) by Tracey Emin, which took the form of a hanging appliquéd blanket.

Above right: **In Grief**
Rozanne Hawksley
1995
Photography: Brian Hawksley

Right: **'I will fly south to the sea and the sun, now my Time has come' – for Matthew 8.1.95 (detail)**
Rozanne Hawksley
480 x 460 x 40mm (18¾ x 18 x 1½ in)
Wood, pastels, silk thread, gilded pins, bone, fabric
Photography: Brian Hawksley

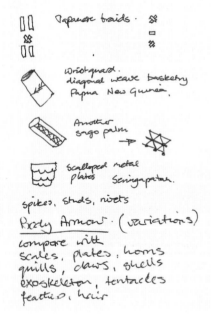

Notebook pages
Penny Burnfield
A5 (148 x 210mm [5¾ x 8¼ in])

Conceptual pieces may include a wide range of media, such as wood, glass, metal and stone, as well as textile and thread. The exploration could also take a wide variety of forms in its presentation; three dimensions and installations in which the piece(s) cross physical space are popular. Sometimes video is used to include a time-based element.

The nature of conceptual pieces will often cross or blur traditional artistic or cultural boundaries. They may also raise questions about the hierarchies of media. It can be that in such pieces the very choice of fabric or thread is the contentious issue. Fabric and thread have such a rich cultural history and the medium exists within the paradox of being both ubiquitous and marginal. The very commonplace nature of textiles and threads can make them difficult to use as a tool for critical, aesthetic practice. The most common cultural boundaries to be challenged by artists using textiles are between fine art and craft, and between masculine and feminine. The direct challenge to perceptions of cultural boundaries may be incidental or deliberate, but the questioning behind the work is what guides the research and exploration.

The sketchbooks by Penny Burnfield demonstrate a particular form of recording thoughts, ideas and working methods that do not rely on drawing. She prefers to describe them as notebooks. The starting point for a particular project might be to 'brainstorm' or 'mind map' by writing down lists of words that are likely to include:

- Any restrictions or criteria for the work, such as size, colour, two or three dimensions, how it will be hung or displayed, whether it will be travelling to various venues
- Key words about the ideas and thoughts being conveyed
- Further sources of research, including museums, books, galleries and people to contact
- Technical points, such as materials and methods of working

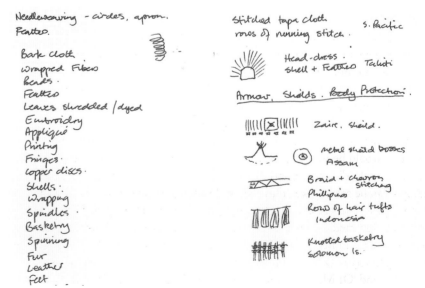

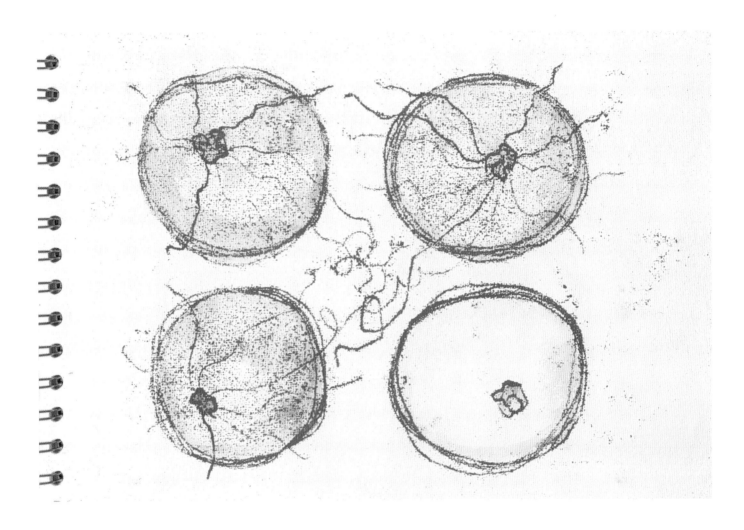

Sketch: Subconscious imagery
Penny Burnfield
A4 (210 x 297mm [8¼ x 11¾in])
Monotype
Photography: Penny Burnfield

These lists are not definitive; they remain open and are added to as she works. Thumbnail sketches sometimes follow them and then possibly working plans, which include dimensions, notes about technical difficulties that need to be considered and how the work will be presented or displayed.

This is a common way of working for many artists who, for one reason or another, do not find direct observational drawing a suitable basis for their ideas or thoughts. For many, it would be impossible to draw what they want to express. For Penny Burnfield, the final artworks have little to do with the observed world and more to do with her interior world of thoughts, or the way society works. Both of these are imprecise, mysterious, or enigmatic non-visual ideas that would be inappropriate to represent in drawings. When Penny draws, she uses simple, direct monoprints, which have a strong, expressive line. An example can be seen above. This way of sketching allows her to work from a spontaneous, subconscious starting point, which often reflects her scientific background in medicine and botany as well as the three-dimensional forms that become evident in her final pieces of work. Such references can be clearly seen in 'Ancient Preserves' (2000) and 'Specimen Collection' (2004), published in 'Art Textiles 2' and 'Of Material Concern' respectively. The themes in these pieces

Holotype
Penny Burnfield
2004
Glass jars, paper, felt, yarn, paints, dyes, shells, labels
Photography: Garrick Palmer

relate to the human need to explore our origins. We collect, categorize and display the relics of our antecedents. Initially amusing and engaging, the work often has a more sinister undertone, raising questions about human nature.

The themes evident in the work already discussed have again come together in a recent piece entitled 'Holotype', pictured above. While researching for an exhibition in the Pitt Rivers Museum, Oxford, Penny discovered, to her delight as a biologist, the adjacent University Museum of Natural History. The associated ideas and title come from the scientific process followed by biologists when they discover a new species. The word describes a single specimen used as the basis of the original published description of a taxonomic species (in other words, the 'original' specimen is always described as a holotype).

Some readers may find it annoying that even though they can see sketchbook pages, these still do not necessarily show a clear progression of ideas of every stage of the process of creating a piece of work. In my experience, these are concepts that cannot be drawn. Scribbles or thumbnail sketches catch some of the more visual ideas, however, and are usually fully annotated (see page 47). They are made wherever I happen to be at the time, on whatever notepaper comes to hand, and then often carried round in the back of my diary, being added to and thought about regularly. I don't put them in my sketchbook, but instead eventually store them in a plastic wallet pinned to the workroom notice board until their time comes. Both the sketches and the ideas are often very private and, indeed, are made only as a reminder to myself. At a later stage, perhaps after several years, they may come together with more formal research and grow into a completed work.

Opposite:
Sketchbook: Underrated Treasures
Kay Greenlees
A3 (297 x 420mm [11¾ x 16½in])
2004
Photography: Jerry Hardman-Jones

The pages reproduced here show the sketchbook being used to record the working process for one textile piece, 'Identikit', in the series 'Underrated Treasures'. These pieces bring together several personal interests. They are inspired generally by the idea of working within a particular museum, the idea of collecting, and my interest, as a design historian, in how we use objects. On the left side of the sketchbook page is a monochrome 'in relief' drawing (or

July 04. Working process + notes for 'needlecase' piece. Searching for ways of making my ideas visual, started by arranging my collection of 'memorabilia', in this case my collection from my 'shrine' to Ganesh - God of opportunity. Items on the far right below. Looking for visual connections between the disparate items, all had interesting surface qualities usually texture, raised or incised surfaces. All were 'found' objects with an individual attraction a 'magpie' like collection of bright, cheerful even gaudy things. After thought collection refined, things removed ~ but could also have added.

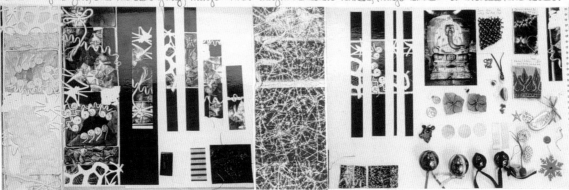

From this collection the surface of the object was 'drawn' or rather re-presented by working in white papers + containing the drawings within a box structure. Far left. This was photocopied; 2nd left and then the copy cut up to offer a design starting point ~ used the black papers as well. Centre right in photo + below right. Not pursued. Looking for a way to present the idea (of collecting needlecraft implements) I used the form of the needlecase itself to explore ideas of individuality in both the collection + the making process. In terms of re-cycled items; hand-me-downs it contains elements of many women's history in relation to the culture of sewing.

Pattern of the needlecase ~ actual size as sold. Pattern twice the size ~ suitable.

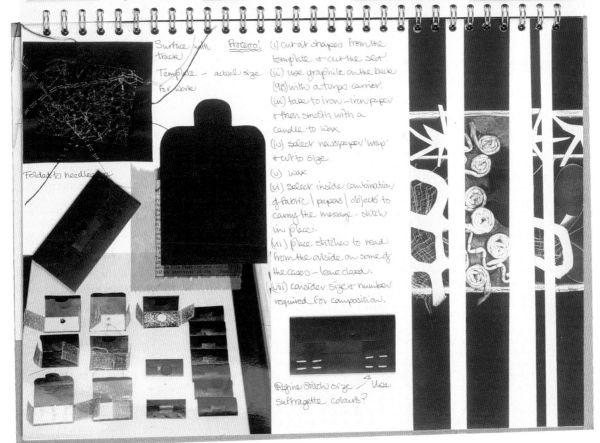

Surface with track
Template ~ actual size for above

Folded to needlecase

Process! (i) cut out shapes from the template + cut the slot.
(ii) use graphite on the back (9B) with a torpos carrier.
(iii) take to iron - iron paper + then smooth with a candle to wax.
(iv) select newspaper 'wrap' + cut to size
(v) wax
(vi) select inside combination of fabric / papers / objects to carry the message - stitch in place.
(vii) place stitches to read from the outside on some of the cases - leave closed.
(viii) consider size + number required for composition.

Refine stitch size ~ Use suffragette colours?

Underrated Treasures (detail)
Kay Greenlees
77 x 64cm (30¼ x 25¼ in)
2004
Waxed papers, fabric, haberdashery, stitch

re-presentation), suggested by the surface qualities observed in a small collection of 'everyday treasures'. These were selected from a small 'shrine' in my workroom and are recorded in the photographs on the right of the page. (I had intended to work from a collection of small antique needlework tools, but on the day the varied 'treasures' were more appealing.) The treasures included shells, pebbles, mah-jong counters, marbles, bits of embroidery and feathers, bottle tops, shoe buckles, flowers and minerals. All of these small pieces have associated personal memories. The monochrome drawing has been recorded by photocopying, and then the copy cut and rearranged to explore possibilities for design. I had no interest in this form of 'translation' into design and looked instead for a way of 'presenting' my ideas about the collection, taking inspiration from the way that items of haberdashery are themselves 'presented' for sale. The needle case form was explored, enlarged and the black photocopy paper used for the prototypes. This has given a very contemporary look to the form of the work. Inside each case is an item of haberdashery. These range from actual antique items, hand-me-downs or inherited things, bric-a-brac and finds from car boot sales, to contemporary buttons from much-loved garments. No matter what the source, each small item has been too precious to be thrown away by its owner and is now re-presented as an underrated treasure. By association, the title invites thought about the countless women who used these once mass-produced items to create items of individual use, beauty or worth. They are in every sense 'underrated treasures'.

In using the sketchbook to record this process, I have been seeking to understand more clearly how my originally non-visual ideas have eventually been visualized. I have become better able to explain the work to myself as well as others, and each time this happens I am able see new things or to see them in a different way. Without the seemingly unconnected 'drawing', the final piece would have lost some of its subtler qualities. It prompted close observation, thought, and the selection and rejection of ideas for a way forward. My current work explores the culture of sewing. The comment(s) I make are not politically contentious, nor are they celebratory. Historically, women have not been well served by their cultural associations with textiles or sewing, and the pieces hint at the paradox that for many of us remains true today. Our very involvement with something that we love and enjoy is often the means by which our contribution to culture remains 'underrated'. I have been tempted here to steal a quotation from Amanda Clayton's collection – 'A woman should never learn to sew – and if she can must not admit to it', taken from the film *The English Patient*.

A different approach to sketching and textile resolutions is seen in the work of Audrey Walker. For 'Observed Incident', she has a range of preliminary studies. Sometimes working in a sketchbook, which she prefers to call a notebook, but more often drawing on a larger scale, she uses these sketches to explore several aspects of the eventual composition. The smaller notebook studies (below) show a quick sketch made in the Victoria and Albert Museum, London, presented alongside other notebook pages developing the idea of the watching figure. Both aspects are developed in larger drawings (above left and right on page 68). None of these correspond directly to the final composition in the panel, which has been allowed to grow and change as the making proceeded.

Preliminary studies for Observed Incident
Audrey Walker
210 x 350mm (8 x 14in)
2002
Ballpoint pen on paper

Above: **Preliminary drawing for Observed Incident:**
Watching Figure
Audrey Walker
350 × 280mm (13¾ × 11in) 2002
Graphite, pastel, charcoal

Right: **Preliminary drawing for Observed Incident**
Audrey Walker
210 × 180mm (8¼ × 7¼in) 2002
From a fragment in the Victoria and Albert Museum

formal
pantcined
stitching
on
column.

important
*
observer?
Angel?
watchman
a quiet pale
figure
frames the stage

very free directions
of stitch.
'free' drawing.

hands, gauntlets
beards. helmets.
shields.

V+A
gallery 101.

English .1380-1410

very complex composition.
gets a whole incident
into a tiny space!

martyrdom of St. Thomas a Becket
(panel from an orphray)

actual size is about ⅕ this drawing.

Above: Observed Incident (detail) *Audrey Walker*
2002

One drawing (above right) is a carefully observed study of a 700-year-old embroidery fragment in the V&A Museum. This has always been a favourite of hers, mostly in admiration of the medieval embroiderer who managed to describe the Martyrdom of Thomas à Becket in an embroidery not much bigger than 10cm (4in) square! Drawing has revealed the subtleties of the composition: overlapping shapes, contrasting rhythms, half-hidden details, hand gestures, facial expressions and a quietly watching figure, which intrigued her. Annotations accompany both sketches, but the drawing also captures the effect of the original stitches. With the silver-gilt worn away, the threads have a new significance for our eyes. The stitching is multi-directional, very free – rather like an etching – and these qualities have been connected to the way that Audrey Walker tries to make her stitching work.

Subsequent notebook studies (page 67) and a larger drawing (above left) show the watching figure gaining importance. The drawings explore various reactions of the observer to the violent incident, the use of the curtain as a compositional and narrative device, and how the observer would connect to us, the viewers. From these preliminary thoughts, she 'plunged in' with fabric and threads and allowed the process of stitching to determine the final work. There are significant developments in the composition of the stitched textile. The gaze of the observer towards the incident is less direct, less active than in the studies and there has been a subconscious return to the 'quiet watchfulness' of the medieval standing figure.

Sketching on location

If sketching is a difficult process for you, then sketching 'in public' can frequently have the added concern of an often inquisitive audience. To add to possible difficulties, the weather may not be good or the museum or gallery may only be able to offer you a half-day appointment to study a particular collection. If you have to travel some distance to reach your chosen location, then you may only be able to afford a day to visit, both in terms of travel costs and accessibility. Many people have the added opportunity to sketch while on holiday, but may still have family and friends to contend with.

These problems are shared by all of us, and the sketchbook is the time-honoured solution to the problem. Working quickly becomes paramount and the use of the sketch really comes into its own in these situations. Refer to the three-minute beach sketch by Audrey Walker (below), which was completed for 'a bit of fun'. Despite its spontaneity, or perhaps because of it, the sketch still records her ongoing interest in the relationship of one figure to another; the glance, the encounter, the observed and the observer, which can be seen in her recent work.

On the Beach sketch
Audrey Walker
A5 (148 x 210mm [5¾ x 8¼ in])
Pen on paper

Out and about

All sorts of locations lend themselves to working with a sketchbook. Try some of these:

- At work: people doing things
- In town: architecture, crowds, patterns of movement, shopping centres, house details
- On holiday
- At home – family, friends, relations, pets, gardens, yards
- Public events – a fair, a boot sale, a carnival, a flower show, concerts
- Building sites – buildings going up or being demolished
- Working buildings – mills, factories
- Gardens – on heritage sites, parks, at home, allotments, botanic gardens
- Aquaria, farms
- Waterways – rivers, canals, docks, the coast
- Activity centres – swimming pools, boating or sailing, ice-rinks
- Markets – open markets, supermarkets, garden centres, flower markets
- Travelling

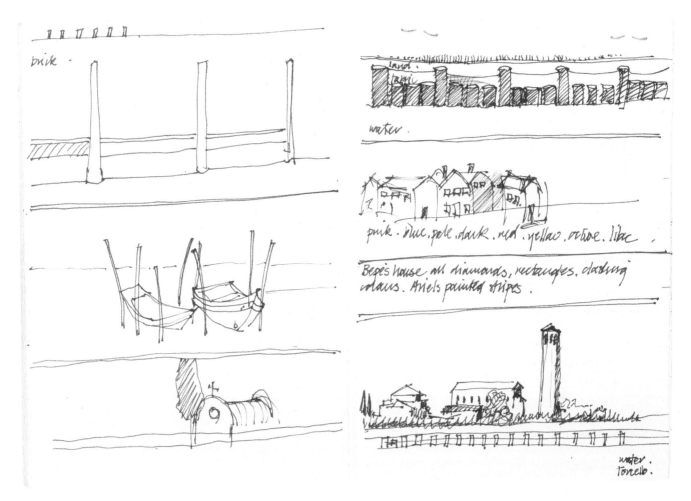

Views from Vaporetto to Torcello.

These immediate yet carefully observed sketches capture the views from a moving *vaparetto* while travelling in Italy. The spontaneous page divisions help record the ever-changing 'snapshot' as the waterbus moves towards its destination. Short annotations help establish details of surface and pattern, including 'brick', 'water' and 'house all diamonds, rectangles and clashing colours.' A sense of place is clearly established by a simple use of line and a storytelling structure.

Travelling: Sketches from a Moving Vaparetto
Sarah Burgess
A6 (105 x 148mm [4 x 5¾in])
Pen on paper

Materials for location work

It is impractical to carry a full kit around with you at all times, so try to limit what you take with you to the bare essentials for the topic you intend to study that day.

Sketchbook A small notebook or sketchbook can be the most useful size to take with you, especially if you need to get used to sketching outdoors. Some people prefer a literal 'pocket book'. The A6 size (105 × 148mm [4 × 5¾in]) is often ideal, but you must feel comfortable with your choice as you develop your

Opposite top:

Sketchbook: Views of the Yorkshire Wolds

Rose Horspool

A5 (148 x 210mm [5³/4 x 8¹/4 in])

Pen and ink, wash

Opposite bottom:

Sketchbook: Landscape from chapel window

Rose Horspool

A4 (210 x 297mm [8¹/4 x 11³/4 in])

Pen and ink, wash, rollerball pen

Below:

Sketchbook: Quick mark-making

Rose Horspool

A4 (210 x 297mm [8¹/4 x 11³/4 in])

Marks to record media and effects

own response to particular situations. A friend with whom I travelled through Russia used a miniature sketchbook and a small watercolour set, the water being carried in a small plastic film container. As you settle into this kind of work you will discover which size and type of sketchbook you prefer.

Drawing media Essential items include a pencil, a pen, an eraser, a pencil sharpener and several paper clips. Details can be found on page 115.

Colour If you would like to introduce colour into your sketchbook, small watercolour sets can easily be purchased. Coloured pencils or aquarelles can be useful, but colour often plays no part in location work: sketches completed in pencil or pen may rely on detail, shape, proportion, line, or patterns. Frequently, written notes are made about colour and added later when time allows.

Carrying your materials A suitable pocket is fine for a small sketchbook, or perhaps a small bag that can be carried across the body and will not interfere with your ability to draw. If you are a collector as well, then a small plastic bag is useful for leaves, tickets, feathers and so on that might be found along the way.

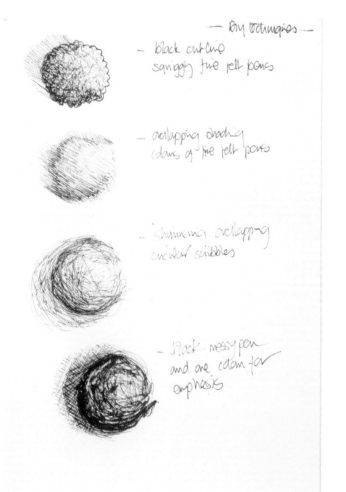

Getting started

Nothing beats getting out there and giving it a go. However, it could be useful to do some timed studies. Examples can be found on page 90. If you are new to quick sketches, this type of experience will help familiarize you with what you get in return for a specific investment of time. Just what do you get from a 2-minute study? Is this useful to you? Why? Do you need longer? Why? What do you get from a 5-minute study or a 20-minute study in comparison?

To put myself in the right frame of mind, sharpen my concentration and help me forget about outside issues, I tend to use a combination of short timed studies. This also serves to remind me of the volume of work I may have accumulated at the end of a day's sketching. This way of thinking is often useful in terms of causing you to appreciate how long it may take to collect and record visual information. This in turn may help you acknowledge your own speed of working, leading to a realistic expectation of whether the day will yield a few pages of work, or a whole sketchbook! How much one produces is not the point, but location work may require a realistic estimate of a time/work ratio if you are to collect the maximum information in what may be a minimum of time.

Always remember that a sketchbook is a personal response, so try not to worry about what onlookers think or, if you are working in a group, the speed at which others work. It is not a competition.

Views of the wolds seen whilst
walking down the lane on previous
page - sketched on a very cold
blustery days - gives feeling of
movement - curved lines - see
variation on a theme notebook
for design ideas based on these
landscapes - reminder of one here.

A few diversionary pages to put the environment
around the chapel in context -
View south from chapel window - same curves round here.

View west from chapel kitchen window - up lane onto
the wolds - wonderful sunsets here and shadows cast
by the horse chestnuts - barn on right recently restored
and now lived in - again lovely curving lines echoing wolds -

Preparing pages

Some people like to prepare pages. Again, this is a personal decision and it may be useful in some circumstances. For example, when you are planning to work in a location that you have already visited before and you have some idea of your focus, it can be useful to prepare pages with a light wash of colour that can be deepened after the location work. Care is needed with this technique. One advantage is that it 'sets the scene' and lessens the fear some people feel when faced with a plain white page. A possible disadvantage is that the colour may be too strong, thus making any pencil lines drawn over the top difficult to see. Pages prepared in this way will also influence any subsequent colour you may need to add. Further details about techniques for this may be found on pages 118–119.

Making marks

Dartmoor sketchbook
Ros Chilcot
A5 (148 x 210mm [5¾ x 8¼in])

If you are frightened about making the first marks and don't want to try timed studies, then it might help to scribble, making random marks. This action can

Summer

The Warren House Inn.

Dartmoor sketchbook
Ros Chilcot
A5 (148 x 210mm [5¾ x 8¼ in])

serve to remind you what kind of marks or lines your pencil or pen makes and it will free your hand as well as your mind. Even experienced artists will use these ways of 'getting into it' as a prelude to more involved drawing.

Preliminary visit

There may be times when it is possible to visit a location before going to sketch. It could be argued that this is a waste of time and effort. On the other hand, it may offer a valuable opportunity to look around thoroughly before making a decision about what to focus on. It helps to get to know the terrain, whether indoors or outdoors. For example, in the case of landscape, this may help establish viewpoints, colour weightings and so on; in the case of museums, archives or heritage sites, it can help by allowing you to view the collections and displays as a holistic presentation. How often has a museum proved to be too big or too exciting, so that you have left feeling exhausted or overwhelmed by the sheer quantity of exciting material and possibilities for development? If it is unlikely that you will return, focus your mind and sketch as you go. If you are

Above:
Dartmoor sketchbook
Ros Chilcot
A5 (148 x 210mm [5³/₄ x 8¹/₄ in])

Right:
Odin's Land
Ros Chilcot
1.82m x 1.2m (6 x 4ft)
2002
Mixed media, painted paper and canvas, stitched marks

Summer

able to return, treating your first visit as reconnaissance can prove worthwhile, allowing you to select which area you will work in when you finally come to make a sketch.

The landscape impressions by Ros Chilcot on pages 74–77 record the sense of place on Dartmoor, Devon. These fleeting glimpses are initially worked by establishing blocks of light and shade to define shape and distance. The sketches are then 'worked up' on return to the studio. Charcoal has been selected for its ability to cover an area with ease and has been sensitively handled to achieve qualities ranging from a soft and muted effect to quite vigorous and strong directional marks, sometimes enhanced by the use of a ball pen. The sketchbook has been dated and records the changes in the landscape across the year. Limited annotations record the precise location, such as 'The Warren House Inn', or the season, 'Summer'. Longer notes often occur on separate pages, including poems and quotations, addresses, suppliers and specific information about chiaroscuro. This is an example of a themed sketchbook. Ros's resolved pieces, such as 'Odin's Land' (shown left), use elements from within the sketches and seek to develop further the sense of place.

Above:
Dartmoor sketchbook
Ros Chilcot
A5 (148 x 210mm [5³/₄ x 8¹/₄ in])

Sketching outdoors

The list on page 70 offers many outdoor locations that can provide exciting visual material. If you are working in public locations, it is often worth checking with the management that it is safe for you to sketch there. If you are planning to sketch as part of a group, then permission must certainly be sought before the activity is organized. Activity centres, shopping centres and other commercial venues especially appreciate this courtesy. When you are selecting a place to sketch, look for:

- People, places and things
- A 'sense of place'
- The way that different qualities of natural light affect how something is seen
- Foreground, middle ground and distance
- Alternative viewpoints
- Colour

Landscapes, seascapes and townscapes can be enormously varied. Each will invoke a specifically appropriate use of language to indicate something subtly

Sketchbook: Byzantine chapel
Julia Caprara
A3 (297 x 420mm [11¾ x 16½in])
Coloured pencil, aquarelle, acrylic wax

Sketchbook: Garden in Corfu
Julia Caprara
A3 (297 x 420mm [11¾ x 16½in])
Coloured pencils, aquarelle

different in terms of location. For instance the terms 'landscape', 'countryside', 'park' and 'garden' indicate fine distinctions, possibly ranging from the panoramic to the domestic or more intimate situation. Identifying what you are interested in might come before you begin sketching, or it might develop and be refined through your sketching. Distance from your work can be beneficial in that it allows you to see it anew. Personal evaluation is necessary, but we can also be very hard on ourselves at times, seeing weaknesses rather than strengths. However, sharing this private work may provide very useful and revealing evaluative comments. Although inquisitive members of the public may be dreaded when you work on location, they can be a tremendous boost to your confidence when they listen politely to what you are interested in and praise the efforts – 'Wow, I could never do that!'

Levens Hall Sketchbook
Rose Horspool
A4 (210 x 297mm [8¼ x 11¾ in])
Hand-coloured photocopies of original drawings,
contextual reference material

A sense of place

The idea of a 'sense of place' may come through words as well as images, and the words may help you to develop colours or atmosphere when you work into the sketch later. 'Damp, mossy and humid' may lead to an entirely different selection of greens than 'dry, crisp, airy and light', but you may only have moved a few yards from inside a wooded area to a view from the edge of a more open vista.

In trying to establish a sense of place, it may be helpful to note and record the following:

- How it makes you feel – comfortable, on edge, frightened, excited, enclosed, cold, happy, oppressed, stunned, elated?
- What contributes to making you feel this way?
- Be aware of sounds, smells, temperatures, textures and atmosphere. Use all the senses.

Concentrating on identifying and capturing a sense of place will help you respond in a more expressive way, thus helping you to develop a personal approach to the special qualities of a particular place. Do you have a favourite place or building? Do you go there often? What is it that attracts you? How will you capture this? No two people will respond in the same way to a place, or record the same features. You may choose to play down certain features and deliberately emphasize others. The emphasis may be intuitive. As Eileen Adams has noted in *Art and the Built Environment*, 'A place is a piece of the whole environment which has been claimed by feelings'.

The garden sketches by Rose Horspool were inspired by the formal topiary planting at Levens Hall. The double page demonstrates a considered use of photocopies of her original A6 black-and-white location sketches, taken from another sketchbook. Here they have been coloured to develop the fantasy atmosphere and the drama of the forms rather than realism. The annotation hints at 'romantic symbolism' and 'mystery and romance' as well as visually noting sculptural relationships to the architecture of Frank O. Gehry. The drawings achieve a sense of wonder, monumentality, form and presence.

Topiary Sketchbook
Rose Horspool
A6 (105 x 148mm [4 x 5¾in])
Rollerball pen on cartridge paper

The handwritten annotation in the sketch reads:

Turquoise string hanging on cherry tree at corner of vineyard – at Poland – another cloudless day – scented and bird song full – Bank holiday of Easter Monday – French out for walks – laughter and chatter – sound of hoopoes calling to each other – newest green of leaves glowing with gold – walnut trees still resolutely bare with the merest fringes of buds bursting out – woodpecker knocking somewhere – blue-tits calling incessantly – saw a swallow tail butterfly over the vines

31·3·97

Above:

Sketchbook: Turquoise string and cherry tree
Rose Horspool
A5 (148 x 210mm [5³/4 x 8¹/4 in])
Gouache, rollerball pen

Opposite top:

Sketchbook: Irises and day lilies
Rose Horspool
A5 (148 x 210mm [5³/4 x 8¹/4 in])
Gouache, rollerball pen

Opposite bottom:

Sketchbook: Clashing tulips
Rose Horspool
A5 (148 x 210mm [5³/4 x 8¹/4 in])
Gouache, rollerball pen

The same artist demonstrates a similar fascination with form and colour in her plant studies. The annotations again provide invaluable information about the experience. I have repeated them here to show how useful they can be.

Top left Turquoise string hanging on a cherry tree at corner of vineyard – another cloudless day – scented and birdsong full – Easter Monday – French out for walks – laughter and chatter – sound of hoopoes calling to each other – newest green of leaves glowing with gold – walnut trees still resolutely bare with the merest fringes of buds bursting out – woodpecker knocking somewhere – blue-tits calling incessantly – saw a swallowtail butterfly over the vines. Love these acidic yellows and brightest blues and greens.

Top right Irises and day lilies at the barn, March 27th. Brilliant spring day – sky as blue as the shadows – countryside iridescent with sunlight – birdsong – tractors – buzzards – woodpeckers – discussion about swimming pools – bells everywhere – wisteria and Rosa banksia out together – scent of apple blossom everywhere – the most beautiful it's ever been here. Could get away with singing colours balanced with greens and cream accents.

Bottom right Wonderful clashing tulips in yellow, magenta and red shapes under the walnut tree at the barn. Linda says this is like a fantasy wallpaper design. Like the arched shapes inside the poppy heads, reminiscent of Paxton's arches at Crystal Palace.

Originally worked separately from the topiary sketches, these studies explore colour separately from form, and provide the inspiration for the colour references made in other areas of the topiary sketchbook.

wires and day lilies
at the Barn, Ireland.
March 27th 1997 brilliant
spring day - sky as blue as here
shadows - complete wonderment
with sunlight - bird song
tractors - vineyards - woodpeckers
discerning about seismic pods
pour Jesus - bees everywhere
madeira and Rosa Banksia Lutea
all together at Ireland - scent of
apple blossom everywhere -
the most beautiful it's ever
been here

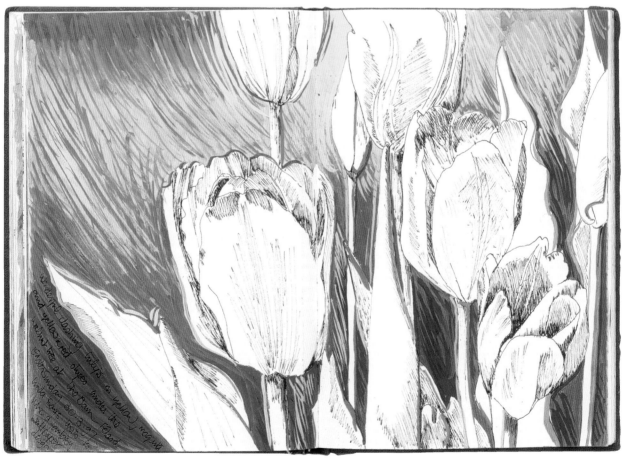

striking dashing tulips in yellow
and yellow-red tinges under the
walnut tree at the Barn Ireland
Banksman 20.3.97
Linda leant 26.4.92
Wine & lamplight
all together
dusk

Observing the landscape

With your basic sketching kit in place, observe your chosen landscape and decide on the area that you want to capture or record. What is it about that area that attracts you? Is it a particular group of trees, field patterns or swathes of open space contrasted with detail, areas of colour, tracks and paths, the depth of a quarry, monumentality of cliff forms, the hugeness or weight of the sky, or simply the atmosphere of the place? If the choice is too great, just begin sketching. Review your work as you progress and then see how well both your pencil studies and your colour notes support your development of the sketch when you return to your working space. As you travel through your landscape, your sketchbook is helping you to map the terrain and record your experiences emotionally, intellectually and visually.

Three sets of work are included here that show different approaches to sketching in the garden. Those by Rose Horspool (page 81) show a clear interest in the 'architectural' appearance of the topiary in the gardens at Levens Hall. This captures its sculptural and monumental qualities, and the sense of space and form the topiary lends to the formal garden surrounding it. Colour is also used imaginatively in these sketches to help capture a sense of place, and the annotations are very important in establishing and later allowing her to re-create the mood on the day.

The set of work by Dorothy Tucker demonstrates a different use of sketching practice in that she develops work prompted by an initial study, which is featured in the embroidery 'Glimpses' (page 87). In this work, a clear sense of place is created by the striking contrast of the glossy greenness of the meadow and the bright yellow of buttercups, glimpsed between the timbers of an old shed. It captures how she was feeling at the time and was worked from memory, feelings and one or two photographs taken from inside the shed and also in the field outside.

Following the completion of 'Glimpses', the artist's fascination with colour mixing and the problems and possibilities of matching fabrics to paints and threads has subsequently been developed in preparation for tutoring a Summer school. Sketches a, b and c (pages 85 and 86) record some of these experiments. These working samples explore mixing acrylic yellow (cadmium yellow deep and cadmium yellow light) with increasing amounts of blue (ultramarine blue) to create greens, and then working free-style stitching into painted cotton twill (b) and muslin (c). The gradations from yellow to green were recorded systematically. To test colour changes, she put brush strokes on paper and later surrounded these with colour washes (a). She also painted patches of colour onto fabrics, initially onto cotton twill (b). The cotton twill was mounted on dyed silk and then stitched into. This was difficult because there were layers of fabric and the cotton twill was stiff with paint. On a single layer of muslin stretched in an embroidery ring, she then experimented further. Using different ratios of paint to water, from very thin washes to thick paint taken directly out of the tube, she then worked free-style embroidery into the painted areas. When stitching was complete, the muslin was mounted on a board covered with white cotton (c).

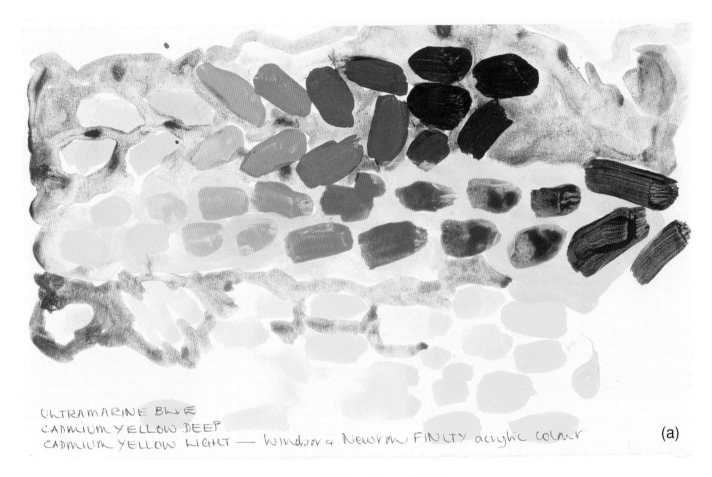

ULTRAMARINE BLUE
CADMIUM YELLOW DEEP
CADMIUM YELLOW LIGHT — Windsor & Newton FINITY acrylic colour

(a)

(b)

Above:

Stitch developments: mixing greens
Dorothy Tucker
240 x 250mm (9½ x 9¾ in)
2002
Acrylic paint on paper, using cadmium yellow deep and cadmium yellow light with increasing amounts of ultramarine blue to create greens

Left:

Stitch developments on fabric
Dorothy Tucker
210 x 140mm (8¼ x 5½ in)
2002
Cotton twill painted with patches of colour, mounted onto dyed silk and stitched

Below:

Stitch developments on fabric

Dorothy Tucker

280 x 170mm (11 x 6¾ in)

2002

Muslin stretched in a ring and painted with thin washes
and impasto. Stitched and mounted over white cotton

(c)

Glimpses
Dorothy Tucker
280 x 280mm (11 x 11in) 2002
Freestyle hand embroidery worked into silks
on torn fragments of fabric mounted
between wood and handmade paper

The sketchbook pictured here has been used to record the 'technical' work related to the exploration of colour mixing. This systematically notes the proportion of blue to yellow in mixing the green, and records this, both in the paint and in the fabric samples, which were dyed with Procion. In theory, if the notes are good it should be possible to re-create the colours should they be needed in greater quantities or in different fabric qualities. The fabrics have been noted for future reference in the book and also left as swatches to be used for sketching.

Sketching indoors

Museums, galleries and archives offer immense potential for researching and developing ideas. Most people have easy access to a local museum or are within a reasonable travelling distance of larger and more specialized archives. Many of these have rich collections of natural history, ethnographic material, textiles, working machinery and countless other exhibits that would serve as starting points. They also generally have handling collections and reserve collections that can be viewed by appointment, in addition to the material on permanent display in the galleries.

Working in a museum – permanent exhibits

In a museum or heritage site, location sketching really comes into its own; photography is often not allowed or, if it is, can be spoilt by the reflections from the glass cabinets and frames. Often, the light levels may be too low to provide a good record of the exhibit and inevitably the museum does not have a postcard of your favourite pieces. This on its own can be an incentive to sketch.

If you are working from the permanent exhibits on display at a museum or gallery, try the following suggestions:

- Make quick sketches, using a pencil to establish the main shapes and areas of detail
- Establish the proportions of the piece you are working from
- Use light and shade to indicate form
- Try different viewpoints of the object
- Use diagrammatic drawings to communicate essential information

- Note colours either in words or with coloured pencils (remember these change if water is added later)
- Write notes to record factual, historical or technical information – for example the date of the piece or the place where it was made or manufactured. Note the name of the place and the gallery you are working in and collect any relevant published material

Working quickly can be quite advantageous. It can build confidence and may result in a bold and decisive way of drawing. Working quickly prevents over-reliance on the use of an eraser or the potentially stultifying tendency to 'polish' the drawing. Even in galleries where all the exhibits are protected by glass, it is unusual that water would be allowed, so coloured pencils can be useful if you have room for them.

Furthering museum or archive study

If you have already visited the museum you may be able to establish a clear focus for subsequent study. Inspired by your initial sketches and keen to research or investigate further, you may want to book an appointment to view items in the reserve collections. This can be frustrating to organize. Many weeks may elapse before you can arrange a time to see the items. 'Behind the scenes work' in museums is often very demanding for staff, who have educational and community groups of all kinds visiting and using the facilities as well as new exhibitions to hang and display. Particular curators or keepers may be needed for the collection to be accessed and these staff may be based across a region rather than in one museum. You will rarely have the opportunity to roam freely through the collections, selecting what you want to study as you go. Rather you will need to tell the staff what you want to research and book and keep the appointment you have made to see these items. It's a good idea to check what the sketching restrictions and working environment will be like when you make the appointment.

Above:
Fabric samples
Kay Greenlees
Silks and cottons dyed with Procion

Left:
Technical notebook and fabrics
Kay Greenlees
A4 (297 x 420mm [11¾ x 16½in])
Paint and dye colour-mixing records

Working with reserve collections

Working with reserve collections always feels like an immense privilege to me, but it is not necessarily a privilege that relates to the actual working conditions, which can vary considerably. Some museums may have a room that can be used for this sort of study (although you may not have exclusive use of it). Others may just be able to clear you a space in the corner of someone's office, in the middle of the storeroom, or in the cellar. The space may not be comfortable, light or warm. However, the staff will always advise you if you ask. In addition, you may not be able to come and go as you please. Clearly there will be security issues when working in areas of the museum to which members of the public do not normally have access. Again, if you are working throughout the day, check in advance with staff what they would like you to do about lunch and other breaks. It can easily be the case, as the saying goes, that 'what you gain on the roundabouts, you lose on the swings'. The more important and precious a collection, the more uncomfortable the working conditions may be.

When studying in a large museum with a rare national collection, I have found myself locked in a very dusty and inhospitable cellar. However, I had absolute freedom while there to select the specimens from the boxes and draw whatever I wanted. I had to work on the floor (there was no other space) and handle the specimens really carefully as they had spines that easily caused quite irritating skin rashes, rather like cactus spines. The use of conservation gloves here protected me as much as the specimens. Staff let me out at lunchtime, collected me from a specific place after lunch, and let me in again. There was no

**Sketchbook: 2-minute and
10-minute timed studies**
Kay Greenlees
A7 (74 x 105mm [2¾ x 4in])

problem with any of this, as I knew the arrangements in advance and therefore wore old clothes with layers I could add to or remove, depending on the temperature of the storage facility. The point is that if you know what the conditions will be like in advance, you can make best use of the opportunity. It's pointless to have to leave early just because you are too cold to work.

Other constraints

As mentioned above, conservation gloves may be required to handle reserve collections. You may need to take your own, although most museums will provide these. If you intend to do a lot of museum study, you may want to add these to your basic kit. You will need to put these on every time you handle an object, but remove them for drawing and sketching, as the gloves need to remain clean. Photography may be possible, but only without flash. Check in advance that you know how to override the automatic flash on your camera. The museum may only allow drawing with a pencil or coloured pencils. Seek the advice of the museum staff when you book the appointment.

Although working with a reserve collection may be restrictive, it can also provide the opportunity to use a larger sketchbook and there may be desks that can provide support for sustained studies. You may also find it useful to have a large magnifying glass with you, especially if drawing detailed items, such as textiles or jewellery, or if you want to record the thread count of the material and the number and size of stitches in a particular motif. Again, the museum may have these available or you may want to add one to your basic kit.

'Handling' collections

Handling collections are also 'reserve' collections, so you will still need an appointment to use them, but often the items are less valuable than the more perfect exhibits in the main cases or in the reserve collection. These items are sometimes incomplete, damaged, or of less high quality than exhibited items. However, their value lies in precisely these attributes and they should always be handled with care and respect. The items may already have started to come apart or have other damage, but it may be possible to gain insights into the way a piece is made or the way it works that one cannot get from complete, perfect or rare items. Occasionally, costume items in handling collections can be tried on.

Museum staff often have a very good knowledge of other local collections and are very willing to share this. Many universities and colleges have archives that can be available for public study. Some are willing to open their reserve collections for 'specialist' audiences, and if you belong to a course or group then it may well be useful to approach a local facility through your group leader or tutor.

Many specialist societies also hold regular study days to specialist facilities or collections. There is often a small charge for this, and non-members may have to pay a little more. Some societies or groups may also have special visits to private collections where everyone shares their knowledge and expertise. Unfortunately, drawing may not be possible under these circumstances. Archives usually operate in the same way as museums, although they may well have more restricted opening hours. Similar restrictions, appointments and working conditions may apply to churches or other indoor venues with precious artefacts.

Sketchbook: Lace studies
Kay Greenlees
A6 (105 x 148mm [4 x 5¾in])

Recording from objects

The following questions may well prompt research from objects that you can see or handle that may complement your sketches. The questions may even suggest further ideas for drawing that you hadn't originally thought of. They were featured in a book called *Learning from Objects*, by Gail Durbin, Sue Morris and Sue Wilkinson, published by English Heritage.

Physical features
- What colour is it?
- What does it smell like?
- What does it sound like?
- What is it made of?
- Is it a natural or manufactured substance?
- Is the object complete?
- Has it been altered, adapted or mended?
- Is it worn?

Construction
- Is it made by hand or machine?
- Was it made in a mould or in pieces?
- How has it been fixed together?

Function
- How has the object been used?
- Has the use changed?

Design
- Does it do the job it was intended to do well?
- Were the best materials used?
- Is it decorated?
- Do you like the way it looks?
- Would other people like it?

Value
- To the people who made it?
- To the people who used it?
- To the people who keep it?
- To you?
- To a bank?
- To a museum?

These questions may not all have relevance, but most of them can be answered by looking and recording in sketch or note form. Others may prompt further ideas for research.

Sketchbook page
Kay Greenlees
A4 (210 x 297mm
[8¼ x 11¾ in])
Indian cloth tassels and
cowries, small square bag

Gaudy colours, especially when alternated or when applied in little pieces of fabric, are powerful deterrents against evil. The most potent colour by far is red. Edges are frequently of fluttering tassels, often as rags, or of fringes which are a natural arcane of the weaving technique. Most powerful of all talismanic additions to embroidery is the cowrie ~ resembling as it does the female vulva, is universally accepted for its magical powers. It was also widely accepted as currency of great value. Cowries feature on accessories and animal trappings from India to Russia.

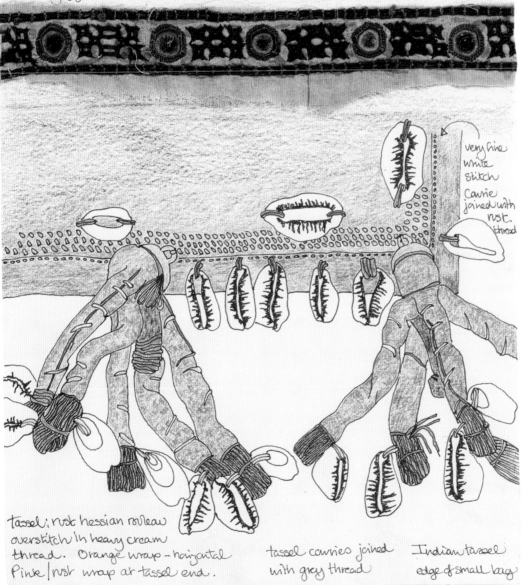

very fine white stitch

Cowrie joined with nst. thread

tassel: nst hessian rouleau overstitch in heavy cream thread. Orange wrap - horizontal Pink/nst wrap at tassel end.

tassel cowries joined with grey thread

Indian tassel edge of small bag

E-sketchbooks

Rapid advances over recent years in computer technology and associated peripherals, such as scanners and digital cameras, have offered us all an alternative to the traditional sketchbook. This causes some serious consideration about the uses of a sketchbook. Does the computer allow the flexibility and portability of the traditional sketchbook? Does it support the review and revision of ideas in the same fluid manner? Does one have the same rapport with a computer sketchbook – that sense of ownership and belonging that artists often build up with their sketchbooks? Or are these facilities and experiences replaced by others that are different but equally valued by those who prefer to work on the computer? As is often the case, what one artist sees as a constraint paradoxically becomes a freedom to a different practitioner.

Portability

Until relatively recently, the computer was a more or less fixed item with little portability. Although lighter and more compact laptops and palm-tops have improved this situation, it still seems unlikely that the computer can offer an alternative to the portability and 'companionship' offered by the sketchbook. Ever smaller digital cameras and recent developments in mobile phone technology have given us the possibility of importing location images directly into a computer. Small DVD recorders also allow the possibility of making a time-based record of any visit or journey that can be edited on screen. These three peripherals all allow the 'location' to be brought directly to the computer and may open up exciting possibilities for location work.

Shoes
Emma Hoult
Image drawn directly in Adobe Photoshop

Barnacle (detail) *Maggie Grey*
Digital camera image exploiting the layers and blending facility of the computer program Paint Shop Pro.

Review and revision

In considering whether the computer allows for the review and revision of ideas in the same way as turning through the pages of a sketchbook, one needs to explore how images can be stored to support the opportunity for reflection and addition. Can several images be seen at once? Doesn't the technology actually make this process more cumbersome? Once you have become a skilled user, the more advanced programs allow images to be grouped so that they can be seen together. To facilitate this, they need to be saved in a named and numbered sequence. This will allow you to find sketches, and the overview allows for some reflection on progress and development.

In the examples by Emma Hoult below, the images have been saved as a group in Photoshop. The illustration shows the layering developments from a scanned museum sketch of a Chinese flower. At this stage, the sketch/design has not been developed because the artist has focused on the layering facility in order to use these for computerized machine embroidery. Sampling would need to be undertaken, evaluated, and the design amended to suit the method of production. The computer can never shortcut these 'trial and error' developmental stages and obviously will not replicate the experience of pinning the samples into your sketchbook. Results from the machine embroidery samples

Chinese flower sketch
Emma Hoult
Sketch scanned and manipulated in Adobe Photoshop

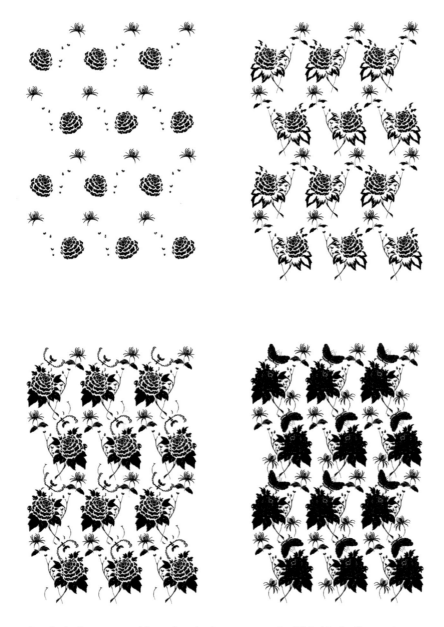

Chinese flower layouts
Emma Hoult
Layers separated using Adobe Photoshop

and technical notes would need to be kept separately. This kind of grouping does, however, offer the opportunity to see several stages of development on screen at once, which gets a little closer to flipping through a sketchbook. Examples shown in the 'Chinese flower' design demonstrate 'layering' used to replicate colour separation in a similar way to silkscreen printing.

Other possibilities for review and revision could be:

- To import drawings/designs into Power Point, which would give another form of presentation, allowing sequence to be shown.
- Alternatively, the flip-chart facility on an interactive whiteboard could provide a similar fluency.

Aspects of viewing and re-viewing sequences prompt further considerations:

• Is the range of marks and effects sufficiently personal or individual? The best work by students or artists questions and challenges the marks offered by the computer and thus extends the possibilities of mark and combinations of effects so that they can have personal meaning and individuality. In 'Boots' by Emma Hoult, below, she makes it clear that she enjoys the fluency of mark offered by directly sketching on the computer rather than the traditional media that she used in the 'Chinese Flowers' sketch.

Boots sketch
Emma Hoult
Image drawn directly in Adobe Photoshop

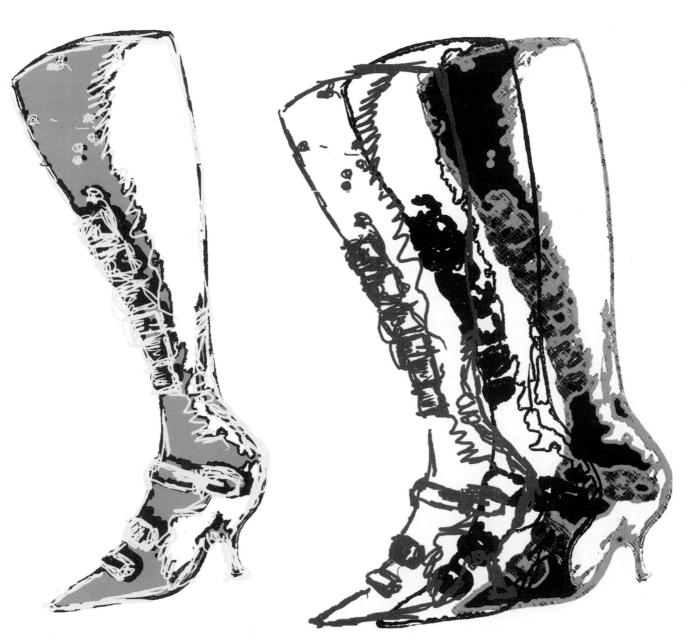

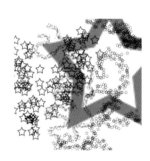

Mark-making
Kirsty Cooper
Worked and presented in Adobe Photoshop

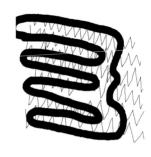

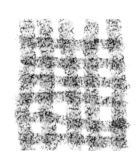

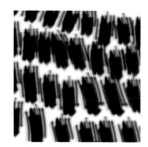

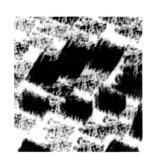

- How easy is it to save various stages of work? What about the size of the memory for storing complex coloured work? With the advent of CD and DVD or saving directly to a memory stick, the size of complex images is no longer a storage problem. The access to those images does, however, remain an issue.
- Does the quality of the printout match the image on the screen? Does this matter? Is the cost restrictive? Does the paper type or quality encourage further working into with traditional media? Of course, the colour match between the screen and print will always differ. The computer deals with coloured light; the printer with inks or dyes. Specialist papers can enhance the quality of the print, but this increases the cost. Traditional sketches are often added to, torn up and repositioned or printed over, but the computer print offers a high-cost finished product, which often discourages further 'working into' with traditional materials. The cost does not deter everyone and Maggie Grey often works up her designs, using pencils, inks, texture media and metallic waxes.
- Does the computer allow for annotation and note-taking alongside the sketching? A sketch process may not be as easily understood, or remembered, without annotation. (Refer to the notes made by Rose Horspool on page 82 and imagine trying to re-create a sense of place without these.) Writing with the mouse can be very cumbersome, but a pen tool on a graph pad can produce text that can be used for annotation. This is not as fluid or fluent as writing in a sketchbook. Annotations can be made by using the flip-chart facility on an interactive whiteboard, although this is no more fluent than using a computer.

Sense of ownership

Enthusiastic sketchbook users do have a great sense of ownership and a rapport with their sketchbooks and this could be similar for those of us with an enthusiasm for drawing on the computer. It is a very different way of working and is likely to appeal to a different type of person than the traditional sketchbook user. Some of the advantages enjoyed by these enthusiasts are mentioned below.

Which program?

If at all possible, it would be advisable to review other people's programs so that you can select one that supports what you want to do, especially before purchasing expensive equipment. Exploring your program is definitely time-consuming and quite frustrating without a 'teacher'. Handbooks do not always make it easy; there isn't always a fault-finder, and it is usually a computer expert rather than an artist who has written the program. It is worth exploring what your computer will already do; simple 'draw' or 'paint' programs are often free with your system. Just as with paper and paint, the complexity of the tool is not necessarily what produces the most exciting or creative work.

Although new programs are being developed all the time, at the moment they fit broadly into two groups.

1. Entertainment-based programs that seek to be fun and to offer 'professional' results for beginners or non-artists. These include features such as clip art and

other entertaining features, such as sound and special effects, as well as a basic painting function. Kid Pix is one such example. Some offer novelty effects so that an initial drawing can be scanned in and then the effect − for example 'pinwheel', 'whirlpool' and others − is applied, essentially rearranging work into complex patterns.

2. Other programs offer no direct correspondence with conventional art practices; here, digital manipulation of data is so different that a whole new range of capabilities becomes possible as the user becomes increasingly expert. Some of the distortion features or 'layering' have no parallel away from the screen. Adobe Photoshop is one such program. It does, however, offer some approximation to conventional tools, such as watercolour, crayon, pastel, pencil, paintbrush, spraycan and erasers, and has a range of effects.

Initial computer exploration often requires a similar personal approach to conventional drawing methods. Trying each tool to see what it has to offer is similar to using a pen to explore a variety of marks, although recording these for future use is sometimes more difficult. Can you replicate an effect? Where do you make the notes that support this experimentation? How sophisticated are the drawing tools? Initially clumsy, the mouse can be manipulated with skill, but some people prefer to sketch on a graph pad with a pen, which is more like a conventional pencil. There is now also a pen for drawing or writing on ordinary

Buddha (detail)
Maggie Grey
Sketch

Buddha
Maggie Grey
Scanned drawing printed out with additional artwork

Buddha
Maggie Grey
Alternatives using the scanned drawing using Paint
Shop Pro

paper, which remembers the movements and can download these into the computer. Most commonly, students or artists scan in their images or part images and then manipulate or draw into them on the computer. Alternatively, designs can be printed out, worked up with inks, dyes or pencils and then re-scanned or effects applied. Scale, repeats, colourways, fills – all can be applied and saved without once having to redraw. Maggie Grey's 'Buddha' series (opposite page and right) is an example of this process. In this sense, the computer facilitates many stages of the design process. Fabric designs can also be seen in the context of a garment or interior.

It is possible that some people who would not use a sketchbook are attracted to using the computer. Often they see it as more fun, offering freedom (not confined by a small page, or waiting for paint to dry). A computer makes it possible to work rapidly and fluently, making clear decisions to save images, and users engage with the process and concentrate on sustained studies. As they are all features of creativity, these working practices are worthwhile. In group situations, moreover, you will often find a willingness to share and communicate excitement about new discoveries and options.

However, some of these features have their limitations. Working rapidly and making clear decisions to save images usually encourages risk-taking, as none of the work needs to be saved at the end of the working session. Revision of the idea or result happens on screen and cannot be viewed retrospectively. This often encourages students to keep only what they like at the time. By comparison, a sketchbook always offers the possibility of reviewing a piece that at first was not liked or was viewed as a failure. It allows the 'failure' to be seen retrospectively as a valuable step on the journey, or to gain its own significance in the light of new experiences. If a sketchbook is required for assessment purposes, an e-sketchbook can be less informative and less accessible than an actual sketchbook. Lack of annotation facilities can also be a problem.

The change in affordable technology is so rapid that all the preceding arguments and points may be eclipsed by a new development before this book even goes to print. However, we do not all have immediate access to the latest technology, or are able to afford the updates and upgrades; the older technologies and software programs remain to be used and the questions remain to be asked of the new systems.

e-portfolios

As e-sketchbooks become more popular, then e-portfolios may also become more commonplace. Currently, these tend to be used as a storage system. A large amount of work can be recorded and a disc is very portable. A CD or DVD can be viewed anywhere that there is a suitable computer and compatible software. Although the quality of the visual image is excellent, does it convey exactly the same things as the original? Will we lose something in this process? Isn't there important information to be gained by seeing work at first hand, 'in the paint' or 'in the cloth'? What does the computer tell us about scale, or surface quality? Aren't we missing something in losing the opportunity to walk around or through installations, to examine pieces close-up, to contemplate, to select our own viewpoint, to concentrate on details or admire workmanship? To touch?

Buddha
Maggie Grey
Alternative using the scanned drawing using Paint Shop Pro

Buddha
Maggie Grey
Alternative using the scanned drawing using Paint Shop Pro

HAWKWOOD.

CHAPTER THREE

MAKING CHOICES: Sketchbook decisions

There are some important sketchbook decisions to be made right from the start.

- Are you making a book or buying one?
- What form will your sketch work take: for example, book, box, computer?
- The scale of sketchbook: will it be beyond the conventional sketchbook?

Purchased or handmade books?

In keeping with most of the advice given in this book, it is entirely up to you whether you choose to buy your sketchbook or make it. As the sketchbook contains some of the most important and exciting work that you will do, perhaps more important than finished pieces, the book that contains these opportunities to reflect, record and analyse should be chosen to support the kind of work that you do. There are a few considerations that you might like to make. With mail order and internet ordering, the availability of a particular make of sketchbook is no longer an issue. Some artists featured in this book have mentioned their favourite working practices. Some of these only ever use the same make and size of sketchbook; others use whatever is to hand regardless of size and scale. Some prefer a stitched spine; others opt for a wire binding. Review your existing books to see if they support your needs. If you worry about filling a page, then perhaps a smaller-sized book would be less daunting.

Handmade book: weathered surfaces of sheds and stables
Mary Youles
210 x 210mm (8¼ x 8¼in) 2004
Reused paper, photography, paint

Considerations might include the following:

Size Select a size suitable for your work – pocket-sized might be easy for carrying, but not all sketching is done on a small scale.

Shape Consider whether you prefer landscape or portrait format. Most sizes can be bought with the binding along the side or the top, although not all may be in stock locally. Alternatively, you may prefer a square format.

Paper The weight and type of paper used can be important. This should be selected to support the medium in which you usually work. Watercolour, pen, collage, the addition of local colour – each may require a different surface, weight or absorbency of paper. A lightly textured surface with sized paper would be most suitable if you work in watercolour. A smoother surface might be more suitable if you prefer to work in biro. A 150 or 160gsm cartridge paper that has a matt surface and is sized for wet media is common to a range of popular brands of sketchbook. In some sketchbooks, information about the paper is printed on a removable flysheet. In others, it is printed on the front or back covers with the maker's logo. Art shops, graphic suppliers, friends and tutors can all be looked to for advice.

Sketchbooks with handmade paper pages are readily available, often with decorative covers. These books may be difficult to use for traditional sketching. Attractive though they are, they may not open flat and the handmade paper is soft, fibrous, slightly fluffy, unsized and very absorbent. This type of book is suitable for notes in biro or ball-tip pens. Gift shops, interior design shops and museum shops often have other attractive books, in a variety of formats, which can be useful. These are often non-standard and can have varied cover treatments and a range of paper types in the pages. Sometimes they are intended as albums and have a lightweight card page instead of paper. The colour of these pages is often not white: beige, brown, grey, terracotta and black are also popular. These can be very useful for drawing and textile work, but they may not be available when you want to replace them.

Bindings The binding might also be important. Spiral bindings can be useful as pages can be removed or can allow for bulk. Tear-off perforated sheets may also be useful. I prefer a 'Wire-o' binding, used by several manufacturers, because the sheets can easily be clipped out of the book and re-inserted. This allows you to work on a page away from the book, which helps when printing or dyeing, and enables you to re-order work at a later date. If the book becomes bulky with collage or fabric samples, it supports the removal of unused pages to allow for the bulk without wastage – the removed pages can simply be added to your new next new sketchbook.

Stitched bindings that open flat have their advantages, allowing you to work right across the spread of pages without interruption. This might be particularly useful for location work or life studies. It may be supportive if your work tends to be flat.

Handmade sketchbooks

Making books has recently grown in popularity and there are a variety of publications on the market that cover all the technical information that you could need if you select this route. Some are listed at the back of this book. A handmade sketchbook can be an exciting alternative to a purchased book, allowing for greater individuality in style, cover, decoration and paper choice. There are a great many ways that books can be bound, decorated and covered, all of which offer creative potential.

Apart from being great fun to make, a handmade sketchbook can encourage a pride in ownership. The personalization begins at the heart of the decision-making process. What size do I want? What format? What type, colour, weight and texture of paper? Will the edges be torn or cut? This personalization tends to be carried through to the work in the book. Some people make their books to support specific research projects. In this process, the crucial question is what do I want to use the book for? Will it be a functional sketchbook? Will it provide a personalized 'presentation' in support of an idea, theme or area of research, or will it take on a life of its own and become a work of art? (It could, of course, start out as one thing and grow into another as you work.) Another question that might be worth considering is whether the book is intended for you, as a gift for others, or as a commercial venture? There are no rules here. At different times your work may go in different directions.

You need to consider very carefully how to decorate your sketchbook, especially if the book is part of the course requirements for art or textile study. Too much concentration on a decorated cover or highly coloured and patterned pages can detract from the content of the book. Ask yourself why you are decorating (or personalizing) the book; what purpose does it serve? Remember that the book is valuable, both to you or an assessor, precisely because it records your own personal thoughts, images, recollections, observations and engagement with ideas or media. The sketchbook needs to be a working document. The content should always be more important than the cover.

Concertina sketchbooks
Kay Greenlees
Pages 100 x 100mm (4 x 4in)
Mark-making for pattern

One of the simplest forms of sketchbook is a basic concertina. These have several advantages:

- You select the size of the 'page'
- You select the paper weight and type
- The book can be extended by simply adding another concertina pleat
- Concertinas are self-supporting, so you can see a progression of ideas
- Edges of pages could be shaped or folds could be cut through
- If the paper is firm, both sides can be used

The two examples shown on page 107 explore the link between mark-making and pattern using the simplest of media: acrylic paint and various brushes (including the wooden end and bristles), and a potato block. Inexpensive and versatile, the concertina method can be used in a variety of situations. It can also provide a good presentational device for displaying sketches completed on separate pieces of paper: 'serial vision' drawings that gradually get closer and closer to a specific focus, for example.

  After a lifetime of using sketchbooks to support research for her textile pieces, Mary Youles has recently turned her attention to the book itself. This has become such an interest that she has attended bookbinding classes and has developed some of her personal books so that the cover complements the subject of the investigation inside.

Handmade books: Fragments of a Working Life
Mary Youles
210 x 210mm (8¼ x 8¼ in)
2004
Denim, reused paper, photographic references

Left:
Sketchbook: cactus studies
Linda Livesey
A4 (210 x 297mm [8¼ in x 11¾ in])

Below left:
Sketchbook: cactus studies
Linda Livesey
A4 (210 x 297mm [8¼ in x 11¾ in])

These remain functional working notebooks. They are themed in their investigation, and the papers are selected to support the practical work prompted by the research. In this case, reused envelopes and brown wrapping papers support and promote the idea of recycling and also of reusing items that have become worn out in their original use. Some of the envelopes provide a printed blue lining that echoes the colour of the much-washed denim. This also promotes the idea of wear and tear observed and recorded on used denim items or the weathering of sheds and stables. Sometimes the envelope sections are used to include a window, thus allowing a view through from one page to the next without cutting into the page. Traditional bookbinding techniques have been used to insert spacers between the pages to allow for bulky or textured work to be carried out without distorting the sketchbook. In one example, reused labels also provide an indexing system for the research. Both books explore the topic 'fragments from a working past'.

Included here are the illustrations of sketchbooks made by Linda Livesey whilst attending a workshop given by Mary Youles. In an extension of her interest in cactus forms, already seen on pages 10 and 11, she makes playful use of the visual and verbal pun 'spine.'

Above:
Handmade books
Linda Livesey
2004

The sketchbook by Jo Owen (left) demonstrates a thorough visual investigation of 'edge qualities', inspired by the Edith Durham collection of Balkan costumes in the Bankfield Museum, Halifax. This themed sketchbook observes, records, stores and develops these ideas. The book shows breadth and depth in its investigation and directly translates this into visual ideas concerned with overlapping, transparency, layering and cut-outs. The book is seen at its best in three-dimensional format. By moving around, it is possible to appreciate the delicacy and the patterns as one page is seen transposed against another. The book format directly supports the exploration and sustained development of the idea of 'layers and edges.' As well as providing valuable research for other pieces of work, the book has itself become a finished piece of work.

Form of sketchbook

What form will your sketchbook take – book, loose-leaf, box or computer? Most of those artists who have given this question some consideration agree that it is precisely the book form that gives the sketchbook its value. We have already mentioned some of the limitations of the computer in allowing the easy review of ideas and developments. The book form, on the other hand, ideally supports this ability to review and revise content. Loose sheets of papers also have their limitations. Although there are occasions when they may be of use, students generally do not value working on paper as highly as working in a book. Additionally, they need to be dated and ordered to support a development of ideas; perhaps too, they make discarding an idea or mark rather too easy. We have already noted that what we once thought were mistakes can prove valuable when viewed retrospectively, or in a changed mood. In this context, the sequence in which work was developed is important for understanding the creative process; failures and successes have equal value.

This is not to say that loose-leaf papers cannot be assembled and added to a sketchbook. Indeed, work developed from a particular idea can be added to in a fold-out format that expands the pages as the ideas grow. This could be in a simple concertina form, or it could open out from a page on all available edges. An example of this can be seen on the opposite page. Siân Martin has used a Japanese child's exercise book, bought from an antique shop in Japan. Even the original red corrections are still in place. Using or retaining the calligraphic script, Siân has inserted her own foldout sections to store and record the developments of ideas gathered on her travels. This includes some photographs of her Shibori samples that would otherwise be too large and heavy for the delicate pages.

Sketchbook: Edge qualities
Jo Owen
430 x 180mm (12 x 7in)
2004
Edges, overlapping, layers, cut-outs

Japan sketchbook
Siân Martin
178 x 229mm (7 x 9in)
2004

Beyond the conventional sketchbook

Moving beyond the traditional boundaries of a sketchbook, the three-dimensional piece by Sarah Hardcastle has become a finished work in its own right, while remaining a progressive piece within a larger body of work. With a brightness of colour and a mixed media cover, it initially has a playful appearance. However, from cover to cover it introduces us to an obsessive-behaviour disorder of turning off electrical switches and the potential fear of the consequences (fire) of not turning them off. As part of a serious exploration of the issue, the features of the book include electrical wiring and components,

Untitled
Sarah Hardcastle
560 x 254 x 305mm (22 x 10 x 12in)
Mixed media, print, stitch, computer drawings

print, stitch, computer drawings and images. Each of the pages must be turned using the various page-turners at the corners; this enforces a more conscious and awkward movement, visually and physically reinforcing the very deliberate process of checking. Although the pages were worked in isolation and then compiled into the book form, the working method has used the idea of vision and re-vision in the same way as working in a sketchbook. The process of working – *pause, record, reflect, move on...* – has been used both as a working method and as a means to compel and engage the curiosity and empathy of the viewer, who also has to pause to 'check' their progress in turning the pages and to reflect before moving on.

This deliberate construction of a book form has allowed the artist the ultimate amount of control over what constitutes a page, what shape the pages should be, what they are made from and what goes onto them. It differs from conventional sketchbook practice in that we do not know if this is a complete record of all the thoughts the artist had as he or she worked through these ideas, or whether a certain amount of selection has already taken place.

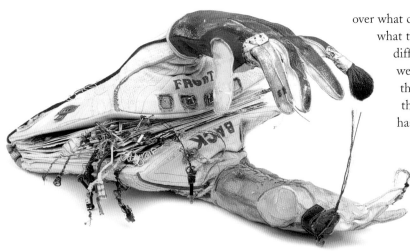

On page 113 we can see another book form used as a presentational format. In this piece of work, Sally E Payne explores and celebrates the lively relationship between herself and her daughter as they dance in the kitchen to the Dixie Chicks, a favourite track being 'Goodbye Earl'. Some of the pages differ in length and width, thus helping to exploit various compositional devices and colour weightings for the edges and sides of the pages, as well as exploring the possibilities of overlapping and overlaying. This allows the viewer multiple 'takes' on the dance,

Child with Untitled
Sally E Payne
2004

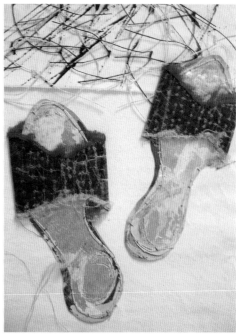

and several aspects can be seen and appreciated in changing contexts. Turning the pages gives a temporal quality that has an alliance to moving through the dance. The narrative of the piece is enhanced by the use of the text 'kitchen dancing, kitchen prancing', by photographs of the dance and by the words to her daughter's own song. Drawn, printed and stitched marks indicating gestures communicate the joy of the shared movement. Printing, combined with transparency, magically captures traces of dancing shoes that have travelled across one page and danced onto another. Despite the size of the book, the format nevertheless assumes the intimacy and informality of a sketchbook by containing 'lots': particular 'takes' on a narrative. Encouraging the viewers to share in the process, this piece has been designed to be seen on the floor rather than on walls.

These examples all demonstrate moves away from the sketchbook as a research tool and towards a resolved piece of work.

Untitled
Sally E Payne
2004
Mixed media, calico, painting, screen printing, paper, stitch, photographs, inks
Photography: Sally E Payne

CHAPTER FOUR

MAKING A START: Technical information

Basic sketching materials

Very basic
- Sketchbook (or just paper), and a ball pen or biro. Give it a go!

Basic
- Sketchbook (size to suit your needs or that you are comfortable with)
- Pencils – HB, hard light – 2B, soft – 4B, softer, darker
- Pencil sharpener
- Ball pen
- Eraser
- Paperclips (10 or so)
- Plastic bags (sandwich bag for found items; or, if outdoors, you may need a plastic sheet or carrier bag to sit on.)

Extensive
- Sketchbook (size to suit your needs or that you are comfortable with)
- Full range of graphite pencils – HB to 8B
- Graphite aquarelle – light, medium, very soft – Karisma
- Coloured aquarelle pencils – water-soluble
- Ball pens – various thicknesses of mark – 0.5, 0.7
- Charcoal and putty rubber
- Fixative
- Wet media, in other words inks/brushes/water container
- Camera and film or digital camera

Sketchbook page
Kay Greenlees
A3 (297 x 420mm [11³/₄ x 16¹/₂ in])
Different kinds of marks

Exploring mark-making

Mark-making is part of our basic visual language. Accidental and random marks, haphazard or scribbled, are the basis of our earliest drawing experiences. Gradually (at whatever age we are when we learn to draw, or when we go back to it after a break), we develop control and ordering and complexity of the marks. Ranging from the tentative or spontaneous, to the careful and deliberate, these marks begin to have meaning.

Once made, the mark becomes an attempt to organize impressions, thoughts, feelings and ideas. Where they are placed and the method used in drawing them transforms the visual field in a series of gestures aimed at identifying the intangible and recording the tangible.

Concentrating on a simple or limited use of materials and on one colour can help focus attention on the possibilities of the chosen combination. This will offer the opportunity to develop an individual mark-making language. Try the following simple experiments.

- See how many different marks you can get from one mark-making tool, such as pencil, pen, brush, stitch, paper, pastels, stick, charcoal, card and others
- Use your 'other' hand
- Explore scale with the marks, and size and speed. Make marks that are thick, thin, graduated, tiny, big, slow, quick, staccato, rhythmic or flowing
- Try combining marks to help describe surface, shape and form
- Try to create a range of tones
- Draw holding two implements at the same time; for example, two pencils or charcoal and pencil
- Explore contrast and repetition
- Make marks by scratching and scoring
- Use basic printing techniques. Cut marks can be made into surfaces for printing – potatoes or lino, for example

Sketchbook pages
Kay Greenlees
A3 (297 x 420mm [11¾ x 16½ in])
Mark as pattern exploring mirroring

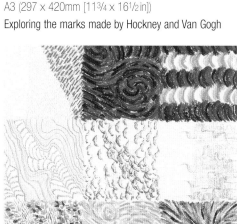

- Try making printed marks on a range of surfaces, which can be inked to provide a strong image or texture (monoprint)
- Draw with a 'mask' or resist, such as masking fluid, masking tape or wax
- Draw by removing a material: removing charcoal with a putty rubber or bread, or graphite with an eraser
- Make marks to respond to music
- Use wet paper. Not only will this absorb media, it can be used for impressed marks as well
- Use a whole range of paper types and colours
- Explore the marks made by other artists; try to re-create these
- Fold, crease, crunch, pleat, stitch paper and then work into it with some of the other techniques

If you are starting out, you could present these experiments in a simple and ever-growing concertina sketchbook, as I have done on page 107. These particular marks were exploring pattern. Can you use any of these marks to complement your sketching and drawing? If you are using a computer as a drawing tool, how does this compare with the quality of marks produced by the traditional media mentioned above? See page 99.

Techniques for colouring pages

Should you colour a background before sketching or after?

Before adding colour to pages, it is worth considering why you might want to do this. It is often suggested that it is a useful way to get started, and there are two reasons why this might be the case.

- Colour might be useful to alter the clean, pristine white page, which for some acts as a barrier to making a mark. Some people feel that the perfection of the page demands a perfect drawing to match.
- It might provide a way of loosening up and freeing the hand and the mind to begin the sketching process. In this way, it can also act to support further drawing and provide a start to a possible free-flow of ideas.

Considering why you want to use colour will help you decide what sort of colour or mark to make. Colour can be very dominant; it can also be very time-consuming to prepare pages in advance of sketching and may defeat the object of having a sketchbook ready to hand. If you want to break up the page before sketching, then some of the following suggestions might be useful. Here, the colour has been kept fairly muted and the techniques simple, so that drawing or note-taking can be made over the top of the colour.

1 and 2. Experiment with inks

Inks used in a random way can give simple but expressive marks. This quality partly results from the lack of control one has in applying the medium. The blue inks have been applied with a dropper onto dry paper and then blown through a straw, the paper being turned to control direction. The green inks have been dropped onto a flooded page that has been allowed to dry a little, letting the ink form interesting blobs. Brush splashes or splatters can also work as well. I like to work over something much more muted in colour. Experiment to see what you enjoy doing.

3. Try water-soluble pencils in graphite form

Experiment with these, as they offer a range of possibilities. As with the coloured aquarelles, marks made with the pencils may disappear once the wash is added, as this will disperse the colour. However, line work can be added over the top with sharpened graphite pencils. The bottom layer shows soft, medium and very soft aquarelle graphite, with a light wash. Tones can be deepened in the same way as the coloured samples. The top layer shows random marks made with a rollerball pen.

4. Begin with drawing inks as a wash

Drawing inks or Brusho colours can be used to provide a range of washes; the colours will blend and run into one another depending on how wet the background paper is. Both these media come in a good range of colours with a fair degree of vibrancy. They can be thinned by the addition of water, thus becoming more muted and suitable for over-drawing at a later stage.

5 and 6. Try water-soluble pencils

Aquarelles or water-soluble pencils come in a wide range of colours and in graphite. Elsewhere, they have been recommended for working on location, where they can be used for museum or landscape colour notes with water being added later, as required. Here, they have been used to demonstrate some

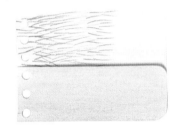

possibilities that can be experimented with further. The bottom layer shows the palest turquoise aquarelle, with the wash applied evenly over the background and marks made by sharpened pencils on top. The second layer shows the same turquoise overlaid and washed successively to build up the colour. These could all make a suitable base for further drawing. In the example above the marks have been applied to white paper and then a wash taken over half the page, demonstrating how some of the marks will disappear and some will blend with each other to give tonal variation.

7. Attempt a rubbing

Two simple rubbings have been included here. These are made with graphite that has then been fixed. Any kind of rubbing will probably give some element of pattern. The technique may be used to create an interesting surface, though it may prove difficult to draw over, with the pattern remaining dominant. I have kept the bottom example unified across the page, but you could keep moving the paper and crayon at different angles to get a more unpredictable or lively result. Any colours could be used. Experiment by rubbing over any item with a sufficiently raised surface and experiment too with the thickness of the paper. Rubbing may be a way of recording 'found' items alongside your sketches. Frottage may be the term used to describe this process, especially when the rubbing is subsequently applied to another surface.

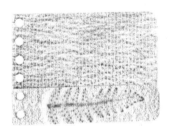

8 and 9. Experiment with sponging

This is a quick and easy way to break up a page. Once again, it can be as muted or as colourful as required. Natural sea sponges give an excellent result, but you can also try decorators' sponges or balls of scrunched paper, such as newspaper, paper towels or bubble wrap. Close tonal ranges can be made or colourful results gained by mixing colours and over-printing. The bolder the

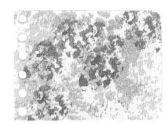

colours, the more they will dominate the page. Completing the page with a light wash can give a more unified result.

10. Use Pantone markers

These random marks have been created with two of the lightest greys in the Pantone range. Each pen comes with two nibs: a wide chisel nib at one end and a fine line marker at the other. The colour range is extensive, the tonal range is good and some colours are strong and vibrant. The bottom layer shows the chisel nib and lightest tone. The second layer shows the same random mark from both the chisel nib and the fine marker in a darker tone. The third layer shows the marks laid side by side; with practice, the colour can be laid more evenly and gives little streaking.

11. Try tea

As a tried and tested way to 'knock back' the whiteness of the page, tea has become ubiquitous, but it can provide a useful range of tones, depending on the strength of the infusion. Other food materials and colourings can also be useful.

Using colour, pattern or texture can also serve to promote the idea being explored in a sketchbook (such as an Egyptian theme), or it can also act as a form of contemplation and enjoyment, as seen in the work of Julia Caprara on page 34. Some of these explorations may go nowhere; some may translate directly into fabric and stitch, and some may influence projects at a future date and time. Try to avoid 'decoration' for its own sake or 'padding out' a sketchbook for assessment purposes. It should not be overworked.

Simple sketchbooks to make

Concertina sketchbook

There are two ways to fold the concertina shape for this sketchbook: one very easy, and one easy. Both alternatives are given in the instructions below.

1. Take a large sheet of A1 cartridge paper (or a paper of your choice) and then fold and cut it lengthways in half.

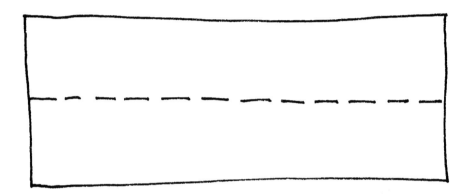

Very easy concertina:

2. Fold in half widthways and then fold each end in to make the concertina shape.

3. Repeat to give added length; trim one end to leave a 1cm (½in) tab for joining.

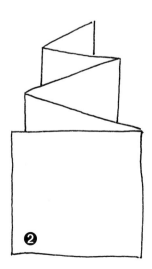

Easy concertina:

2. Mark off the required size of each page along the length of the paper. Fold the paper alternately one way and the other along the lines to make the concertina shape.

3. Trim the end, leaving a 1cm (½in) tab for joining.

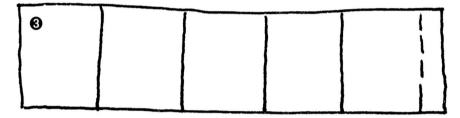

Joining

4. Make as many lengths as you like using either of these two methods, and join them with PVA (white craft glue) or other adhesive. Allow to dry. Press under a heavy weight to get crisp edges.

Adding covered boards

The concertina may be used as it is, or you might want to add boards:

5. Cut a piece of board 2–5mm (¹⁄₁₂–¼ in) bigger than a single concertina page.

6. Cut a piece of cover paper 2cm (¾in) larger than the board in each direction.

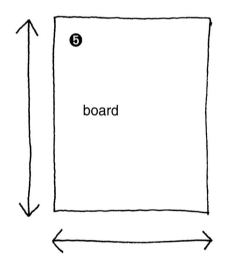
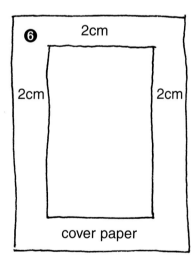

7. Glue the board and stick to the cover paper, folding the edges down. Rub the surface gently with fingers or a spoon to remove air bubbles.

8. Glue an endpaper to the cover, on top of the wrong side, if required, 2mm (¹⁄₁₂ in) smaller all round than the board.

plus 2mm or 5mm

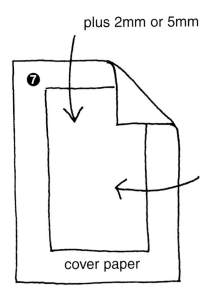

cover paper

9. Glue a concertina page to the cover. This may mean trimming one sheet from your concertina so that it retains its shape when the cover is attached to each end. There should be an uneven number of pages facing you. Insert ties between the cover and the page if you want them.

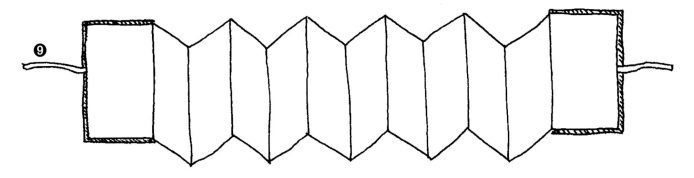

10. Experiment! If you are using this for sketching, generating ideas, having fun, then make several concertinas to keep you going and extend the length as you work. Add the covers only when you have finished.

Try other options as well.
- Work with shaped top edges.
- Explore cutting shapes through pages or through the folds.
- Use both sides.

Concertinas can be good for exploring journeys, time, sequence or pattern. Made from firm card they can be useful for presenting textile or mixed-media samples or experiments.

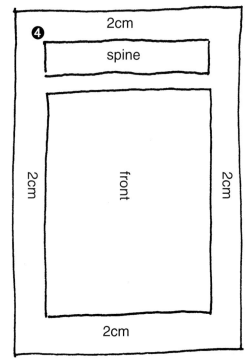

Simple sketchbook with cover and spine

For this more traditional sketchbook, you will require the following materials:

- Thick card for the cover
- Paper for the pages: anything of appropriate weight and surface quality; you could try cartridge paper, wrapping paper or reused papers such as envelopes or handmade papers or a mixture of papers
- PVA adhesive (white craft glue)
- Paper for the cover: choose a soft paper that can be smoothed out and will not leave bubbles on the surface

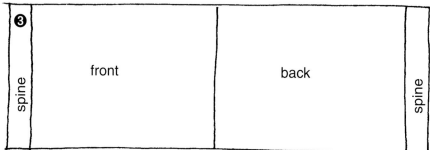

1. Fold the pages in half – as many as you wish and the size that you wish.

2. Cut two pieces of thick card, 2cm (¾ in) larger all round than the pages.

3. Cut off a 2.5cm (1in) strip for the spine.

4. Place card on cover paper, leaving a 5mm (¼ in) gap between the spine and the cover. Have cover paper 2cm (¾ in) larger all around than the cover.

5. Glue in place, leaving margins free. Use fingers, spoon or rag to smooth out.

6. Fold corners over and secure with glue (do not cut across).

7. Fold margins over and glue in place.

8. When they are all dry, line each piece of the cover, pressing the paper well into the 'ditch' between the spine and the cover.

9. Punch holes in the spine, matching them carefully.

10. Punch the pages to match.

11. Thread a cord or ribbon through and pull tightly – finish with a bow, tassel or found object.

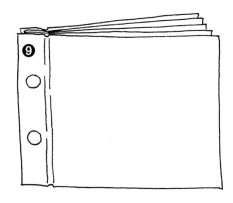

POSTSCRIPT

Many artists have explained why sketchbooks are important for them. Picasso famously used the words '*Je suis le cahier*' ('I am the sketchbook') on the front cover of one of his. Giving primary importance to sketchbook practice, he also said '...I picked up my sketchbooks daily, saying to myself "What will I learn of myself that I didn't know?"'

Your sketchbooks should primarily be for you, but even if yours is part of a course, remember that it is valuable precisely because it records your own personal thoughts, images, recollections, observations and engagement with ideas and media. Try to see your books as part of a journey, or an adventure. Claude Picasso, writing of his father's sketchbooks, said:

> 'They are, from one page to the next, from cover to cover, an adventure – a diary of the painter, the layers of paint, thin or heavy-brooding or jolly on a canvas. They are the notes working up to something or bouncing off something else, perhaps a sculpture into a painting and back. The pages of the notebooks are the sketches for paintings but they are also often afterwords. Sometimes they stand as elaborate works on their own. Picasso's notebooks are stepping-stones to trampolines for somersaults.'

Sketchbooks are an essential tool for an artist or maker. You may find it annoying that, even though you can see a variety of sketchbook practices illustrated here, these still do not necessarily show a clear progression of ideas of every stage of the process of creating a piece of work. In reality, most artists have several places in the process from sketch to final work where there are intuitive leaps – ideas that seem to spring from nowhere in contrast to ideas that steadily grow and change as the piece comes together. Opportunities for reflection, re-vision and evaluation are important. Creativity in the making stage is also paramount. This flexibility, creativity or struggle is vital to the life of the work.

Bibliography

Adams, E and Baynes, K. *Power Drawing*,
September 2001
Adams, E. *Start Drawing!*, September 2002
Adams, E and Baynes, K. *Drawing on Experience*,
March 2003
Adams, E and Baynes, K. *Power Drawing Notebooks*,
December 2003
Adams, E and Baynes, K. *Power Drawing: Space and Place*,
June 2004
All the above are leaflets, published by Drawing Power,
Campaign for Drawing, and are available from
Featherstone Education. PO Box 6350, Lutterworth,
LE17 6ZA (www.featherstone.uk.com)

Adams, Eileen and Ward, Colin. *Art and the Built
Environment*, Longman, 1982
Dunn, Chris. *Art and Design: Sculpture and Ceramics*,
Hodder and Stoughton, 1995
Durbin, Gill, Morris, Sue and Wilkinson, Sue *A Teacher's
Guide to Learning From Objects*, English Heritage, 1990
Glimcher. A and Glimcher. M. Eds. *The Sketchbooks of
Picasso*, Thames and Hudson, 1986
Goldsworthy, Andy. *Time 2000* (with chronology by
Terry Friedman), Thames and Hudson, 2000
Goldsworthy, Andy. *Hand to Earth: Andy Goldsworthy
Sculpture 1976-1990*, The Henry Moore Centre for the
Study of Sculpture, W.S. Maney, Leeds, 1991
Hockney, David. *Travels with Pen, Pencil and Ink*. The
Petersburg Press, 1978
Moore, Henry. *Henry Moore's Sheep Sketchbook*, Thames
and Hudson, 1972
Sparkes, Roy. *Teaching Art Basics*, Batsford, 1973

Catalogues
Art Textiles 2, British Touring Exhibition, 2002–3, Bury
St Edmunds Art Gallery
'Of Material Concern', The 62 Group of Textile Artists,
Sheffield Millennium Galleries
World of Embroidery , Vol 48, No 4, July 1997,
Embroiderers' Guild
'A Space Odyssey', Amanda Clayton and Vivien Prideaux

Further Reading

Art Textiles of the World (Japan, USA, Great Britain,
Scandinavia or any from the series), Telos Art Publishing
Portfolio Collection (features individual 'textile' artists from
around the world, working in a variety of ways – weave,
embroidery, paper, quilt and more), Telos Art Publishing
Reinventing Textiles (illustrations and writings concerning
issues such as identity, migration and sexuality), Telos
Art Publishing.
These titles are all available from:
Telos Art Publishing
Brighton Media Centre
68 Middle Street
Brighton BN1 1AL
01273 201339
www.telos.net

Beaney, Jan and Littlejohn, Jean. *Stitch Magic*, Batsford,
1999
Box, Richard. *Drawing and Design for Embroidery*,
Batsford, 1989
Delamare, François and Guineau, Bertrand. *Colour:
Making and Using Dyes and Pigments*, Thames and
Hudson, 2002
Edwards, Betty. *Drawing on the Right Side of the Brain*,
Fontana/Collins, 1979
Ikegami, Koijiro. *Japanese Bookbinding; instructions from a
master craftsman*, Weatherill, 1986
La Plantz, Shereen. *Cover to Cover – Creative Techniques
for Making Beautiful Books, Journals and Albums*, Lark
Books, 1995
Laury, Jean Ray. *Imagery on Fabric*, C and T Publishing,
1997
Saxton, C. (consultant editor) *Art School*, Macmillan, 1981
Scott, Jac. *Textile Perspectives in Mixed-Media Sculpture*,
The Crowood Press, 2003
Shepherd, Rob. *Handmade Books*, Search Press, 1994
Smith, Stan. *Sketching and Drawing*, Eagle Editions, 2004
Wells, Kate. *Fabric Dyeing and Printing*, Conran Octopus,
1997

Magazines/Journals
Selvedge
P.O.Box 40038
London N6 5UW
www.selvedge.org

Crafts
Crafts Subscription Department
44a Pentonville Road
Islington
London N1 9BY
Tel: 020 7806 2542
www.craftscouncil.org.uk/magazine

Suppliers

Variegations
Rose Cottage
Harper Royd Lane
Norland
Halifax
West Yorkshire HX6 3QQ
Tel: 01422 832411
www.variegations.com
For fabrics, paints dyes, threads

Rainbow Silks
6 Wheelers Yard
High Street
Great Missenden
Buckinghamshire HP16 0AL
Tel: 01494 862 111
www.rainbowsilks.co.uk

Art Van Go
The Studios
1 Stevenage Road
Knebworth
Hertfordshire SG3 6RE
Tel: 01438 814946
www.artvango.co.uk

Seawhite of Brighton
Star Road Trading Estate
Partridge Green
West Sussex RH13 8RA
Tel: 01403 711 633
www.seawhite.co.uk
For sketchbooks and other art materials

Whaleys (Bradford) Ltd
Horton Court
Great Horton
Bradford
West Yorkshire BD7 4EQ
Tel: 01274 576 718
www. whaleys-bradford.ltd.uk
Mail order: mainly plain, undyed fabrics

Societies and Groups

The Textile Society
www.textilesociety.org.uk

The Embroiderers' Guild
www.embroiderersguild.com

The Quilters' Guild
www.quiltersguild.org.uk

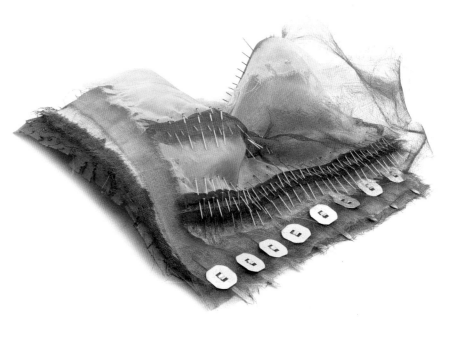

INDEX

Entries in **bold** refer to illustrations.